Behind the Scenes
New Scriptwriting from Bath Spa University

Published by the Bath Spa University Presses, Newton Park, Bath BA2 9BN, United Kingdom, in April 2012

Cover design by Callum Robey
Project managed by Caroline Harris for Harris + Wilson
Printed and bound in the UK by CPI Antony Rowe Ltd, Chippenham, Wiltshire

Sponsored by the Bath Spa University Research Centre for Creative Writing

Behind the Scenes

New Scriptwriting from Bath Spa University

Edited by Hannah Willcock

Contents

Acknowledgements

We would like to extend our sincere gratitude to all those who have made this anthology possible; Dr Steve May, Head of Creative Writing at Bath Spa University; Ursula Rani Sarma, MA Scriptwriting Programme Leader, and Caroline Harris, Project Manager, for her patience and commitment.

Our thanks also goes to Nicola Presley for copyediting; Clive Wilson for typesetting; Jennifer Moore for proofreading; Matt Robertson and his team for providing us with a fantastic range of artwork, and Callum Robey for designing a very fitting front cover.

Finally, a great deal of gratitude is reserved for our tutors: Suzanne Bell, Doug Chamberlain, Hattie Naylor, Jonathan Neale, Robin Mukherjee, and last, but not least, Ursula, for your invaluable help and much appreciated guidance.

Foreword

Scriptwriting is unlike any other form of Creative Writing. Unlike authors who write prose and poetry, scriptwriters produce texts that are only the beginning of a much larger and collaborative process. While we are busy building up our worlds and characters, we know that eventually we will have to hand over this 'blueprint' of sorts to a multitude of varied creative minds. Each of these individuals will interpret the script in their own way, creating an end product, which at times is vastly different to the one which the scriptwriter originally envisioned. Over the course of their time at Bath Spa University studying the MA Scriptwriting, these eight students have worked incredibly hard to understand this particular process and to produce high-quality scripts for the theatre, radio and for screen. They experienced first hand the pressure of having to write and rewrite within tight time constraints, in preparation for the professional contracts they now hope to earn.

Each writer's work is different, however one element that I find consistent throughout is a vibrant and original imaginative flair. From the weird and wonderful setting of Shannon Tweed's *Bright-Line* to the magical and supernatural tale of a little girl who has lost her stories in Lucy Lott's *Grandpa Egg and the Lostgotten*, each of these scripts brings a vivid and whole universe to life within its pages. Hannah Willcock's *Postman's Knock* explores what happens when a young man allows his obsession with time to rule his life, while Peg Killian's *Grace* examines the idea of internal and external beauty. Tina Jenkins tackles the difficult territory of racial prejudice in *Behind the Truth*, while Rob Jennings creates a detailed and intricate landscape inhabited by memorable characters in *North of Tarragon*. Tim Crick brings us on a thrilling journey in *Feedback*, as an ex-soldier searches for the truth of his wife's death, while Patrick Polletti's *Reset Button* introduces us to a dysfunctional family and business in suburban Chicago. What you will find here is the first ten pages of each of these scripts, just enough to get a flavour of these new worlds and hopefully to make you want to read more.

I hope you enjoy reading these extracts as much as I have enjoyed teaching their authors.

Ursula Rani Sarma, Course Leader, MA Scriptwriting

Timothy Crick

Timothy Crick is a published academic author in film and philosophy. Born and raised in Bristol, he graduated from the University of the West of England in 2008 with a first class honours degree in Film Studies, and was awarded first prize for his dissertation. Since then he has channelled his energies and passion into writing screenplays that are mostly in the crime and science fiction genres.

Feedback

This extract is the opening ten pages of *Feedback*, his first feature-length screenplay. Greatly influenced by the works of Raymond Chandler and Alfred Hitchcock, it introduces Daniel Connick, an insurance investigator who finds himself swept into a deadly maelstrom of secrets and subterfuge when he seeks out the truth behind the road accident which killed his wife.

Feedback

Written by
Timothy Crick

Timothy Crick
timharley@gmail.com

INT. MILITARY LABORATORY - OBSERVATION ROOM - DAY

A LOUD HUMMING. INTENSE. THROBBING.

A group of a dozen or so MEN, most of whom wear white
lab coats.

Their faces are lit by a bluish-red glow and their
eyes are wide with wonder. All their attention is
riveted on an event which takes place on the other
side of a HUGE GLASS WINDOW.

The HUMMING grows louder. One of the WHITE COATS turns
his head and looks to the back of the room, where
several CONSOLE TECHIES monitor and direct
the proceedings.

The room is starting to SHAKE a little ... A can
of Coca-Cola starts to move across a desk near the
MAIN CONSOLE. A HAND reaches down and takes the can.
The hand belongs to WILLIAM MURDSTONE (65), a tall
white-haired man in an elegantly cut suit.

He takes a swig, then turns to a CONSOLE TECHIE.

                    MURDSTONE
                 (American accent)
            OK, shut it down. Show's over.

The console techie hits a command on a computer. The
bluish-red light recedes. The SHAKING STOPS. The HUM
fades down to silence ...

EXT. MOTORWAY - NIGHT

CREDITS BEGIN OVER —

We are underneath a vehicle, gliding down a rain-swept
motorway, listening to the rhythmic swish of tyres on
wet tarmac.

INT. CAR - NIGHT - MONTAGE

A SERIES OF SHOTS:

The backs of two people in the front seat — a WOMAN, blonde, driving, and a MAN next to her, dark hair.

Headlights sweep past, flaring across the rain-splattered windscreen.

The road's vanishing point, framed through the rear window. The reflections of car headlights flow like liquid along the windscreen glass. The effect is surreal and dreamy.

The woman reaches forward and puts her hand on the BMW logoed gear-stick. The back of her hand brushes against his leg.

He reaches his hand out to hers. She takes it, holding it gently on her lap. We notice a wedding ring on her finger.

A newspaper, which he's not reading, lies on his knees. The headline reads, 'Earthquake Rocks Swindon'.

A MOBILE PHONE RINGS.

The man reaches into his pocket.

                    MAN
               (looks at phone)
          Withheld number.
               (snaps it open, places it to
               his ear)
          Hello, hello ... I can hear you
          breathing, who is this?

He snaps the phone shut, shakes his head, then settles back into the seat, resting his head against the window.

DRIVER'S POV:

A road sign to Central London; the TICKING of the car's indicator.

EXT. LONDON STREET - DAWN

A Pakistani BOY sits on the window ledge of a newsagent's shop, spinning a yo-yo. He's about 15 years old, oiled hair.

He tries a couple of yo-yo tricks. One of which is a 'sleeper', allowing the yo-yo to sit at the bottom of the string.

CLOSE-UP on the yo-yo. The flat spool has a twirling corkscrew pattern.

We hear FOOTSTEPS RUNNING, drawing closer.

We catch a glimpse of a woman's black low-heel shoes as she sprints past the boy.

The boy's puzzled gaze follows her movements.

More FOOTSTEPS follow, louder and heavier than the first.

We catch a glimpse of a man's black boots as he charges after the woman.

Car headlights approach from down the street. We notice that they belong to a SILVER BMW as it drives past the boy.

Tyres SCREECH, followed by a LOUD CRASH.

The boy's puzzled expression changes to one of concern.

The BMW lies embedded into an appliance store window, its engine wreathed in smoke.

The boy stands, throws the yo-yo on the ground and sprints towards the car.

Amidst smoke and carnage, a young woman's body lies face down on the road near the car. She wears a long black coat and black low-heel shoes. A pool of BLOOD spreads out from underneath her.

The boy runs toward the car and stops. He stands helplessly.

A few curious onlookers begin to gather.

Approaching SIRENS as we rise slowly up over the street. CREDITS END as we —

INT. HOSPITAL WARD - NIGHT

A female DOCTOR and TWO MEDICS stand over a patient strapped down to a rolling stretcher.

> DOCTOR
> (soft)
> Can you hear me? Are you conscious?

The patient is DANIEL CONNICK, late 30s, dark features with a trimmed beard. A cervical collar supports his neck and head.

He blinks painfully as his eyes adjust to the light.

His POV: The doctor looks down on him. There are white curtains and medical equipment in the blurry background.

EXTREME CLOSE-UP of his eye, in which we see the doctor's reflection.

> DOCTOR (CONT'D)
> OK Daniel, we're just going to remove
> your collar and you just lie nice and
> still for me.

As she removes the collar —

                    DOCTOR (CONT'D)
              Any pain?

                    DAN
              (reaching towards the doctor and
              grabbing her arm)
              My wife. Where is she?

INT. DAN'S FLAT - DAY - SEVERAL WEEKS LATER

A large double bedroom. The flat is quiet. Only a
ticking clock.

On top of the dressing table sit various framed PHOTOS
of Dan and a BLONDE WOMAN. Another photo is of Dan in
an army uniform, posing with some army buddies.

In front of the photos lies a clear PLASTIC BAG. We
can't discern the exact contents, but it appears to
contain various personal items: a woman's watch, a
phone, earrings, a ring.

Dan sits on the bed facing a wardrobe. He gets up and,
with a great deal of uncertainty, opens the wardrobe
and stares at the hanging dresses.

He reaches out and pulls the cloth of a red dress
towards him.

The phone RINGS.

He doesn't move to get it. He just stares at it.
Finally he reaches over, picks up.

                    DAN
              (into phone)
              Hello ... Yeah, who's this?

Dan listens. His expression suggests the news isn't good.

                    DAN (CONT'D)
                   (into phone)
              Sorry, say that again.

INT. POLICE STATION - HALLWAY - DAY (A FEW DAYS LATER)

PHONES RINGING. Police officers. The usual.

The front door opens and Dan enters, carrying a small
stack of papers. He still moves like the soldier he
once was, but he's a little thin and pale, and you
can tell by his eyes that he hasn't had a good night's
sleep in weeks.

As he approaches the front desk, the uniformed officer
behind it looks up.

                    DAN
              I need to speak to DI Green.

INT. POLICE STATION - DETECTIVE'S OFFICE -
MOMENTS LATER

Dan sits across the desk from DETECTIVE INSPECTOR
GREEN (55): A paunchy and bald man. On the desk are
the small stack of papers.

INSERT: TIGHT ON PAPERS

The top sheet's title reads, 'Accident Report Form'.

                    DAN
              Is he the only witness you have?

                    GREEN
              We're appealing for more. It was 5:30
              in the morning.

Dan glares at him and pushes the papers aside angrily.

                    DAN
She wouldn't drive like that. Show me
the CCTV footage.

                    GREEN
The Highways Agency are assisting us
with that. She was over the limit,
Mr Connick.

                    DAN
          (through gritted teeth)
And like I told you, she didn't
drink.

                    GREEN
          (referring to a file)
She had ... 96 milligrammes of
alcohol in 100 millilitres of blood.

                    DAN
She didn't drink alcohol. Ask anyone.

                    GREEN
The legal limit is 80 milligrammes.

                    DAN
I can't make myself any clearer.

                    GREEN
          (referring to the file)
So this blood test is wrong? Is that
what you're saying?

                    DAN
Well put it this way, if it's not
wrong, Sarah managed to keep her
little drinking habit a secret for
ten years.
          (struggling to contain his anger)
Is that what you're saying, Detective?
That I didn't know my own wife?

EXT. / INT. CENTRAL LONDON / CAR - DAY - LATER

Dan drives. His face is expressionless.

He hits the indicator and pulls to the curb.
Out of the window he looks across the street at where
several bouquets of mostly withered flowers are laid
at the roadside.

After a moment, he reaches to the passenger seat
and grabs a sheaf of white lilies. He climbs out
of the car and places them with the other flowers at
the roadside.

He begins to inspect the various bouquets of flowers.

CLOSE ANGLE on a fresh BOUQUET of yellow
chrysanthemums, attached to which is a
handwritten card.

Dan picks up the bouquet, looks at the card.

INSERT: TIGHT ON CARD

There is something written in Chinese and, 'When the
way comes to an end, then change. Having changed, you
pass through. Missing you always, Susie.'

INT. DAN'S FLAT - THE NEXT MORNING

Dan sits alone in his living room, half-watching
a news report about a recent earthquake in
Southern California.

He hears a car pull up outside. Gets up and goes to
the window, looking out.

EXT. NEIGHBORHOOD - DAY - LONG SHOT

A BLACK LEXUS pulls over and parks across the road.
Rain splatters on the dark-tinted windows.

A MAN climbs out of the driver's seat. He carefully avoids the muddy areas to save his perfectly cut suit.

After a short moment, DI Green climbs out of the passenger side and the two men make their way towards the entrance to Dan's building.

INT. ENTRANCE HALL - DAY - MOMENTS LATER

Dan opens the door to find the two men standing at the entrance.

> GREEN
> Mr Connick, hello again. Can we
> come in?

The other man is MARK DAYTON (35). He is smaller than Green, with grey-blond hair and a bold moustache. While his suit is impeccable, it doesn't sit well on his very muscular body.

Dan stares at them for a moment. Nobody even attempts to shake hands.

INT. DAN'S FLAT - DAY - A BIT LATER

Green and Dayton sit in the living-room. Their eyes are glued to Dan as he opens the window and then takes a packet of cigarettes off the end table.

He takes one out, offers the packet to the two men, who both shake their heads.

Dan goes to light up, but each time he tries, he stops to speak —

> DAN
> She can't have stepped out.
> Sarah would have seen her.

                    GREEN
          So you're saying she ran out?

                    DAN
          I didn't say that.

                    GREEN
          So what do you remember?

                    DAN
          Whatever I say is irrelevant.

                    DAYTON
          Irrelevant?

                    DAN
          How can I remember something when I
          was sleeping?

                    GREEN
          But you woke when she hit the brakes?

                    DAN
          Why don't you tell me what this
          is about?

A pause. Dan finally lights up.

                    DAYTON
          Take as much time as you need, Mr
          Connick. But let's go through it one
          more time, and see what is relevant.

                    DAN
          I didn't catch your name. I know
          his, but yours has managed to elude
          me somehow.

Dayton looks at Dan with a calm, unblinking,
unwavering stare.

>   DAYTON
> Dayton. Officer Mark Dayton.

>   DAN
> Which force?

>   DAYTON
> Sorry?

>   DAN
> Which force do you work for? I know
> it can't be London Met, not with a
> car like that.

Dayton looks from Dan to Green, who nods.
A little uneasy.

>   DAYTON
> You work in the private detective
> business, Mr Connick?

>   DAN
> Not exactly. I mostly do insurance
> claims ...
>   (moving to the window)
> That is your car? The black Lexus.
>   DAYTON
> Mr Connick. Sit down please,
> will you?

>   DAN
> They're OK, but one of their problems
> - like most Japanese cars - is
> they're a bit faceless and bland,
> or even ...
>   (turns to Dayton)
> Anonymous, you know?

>   DAYTON
>   (pulls out his badge)
> Please - sit down.

INSERT: TIGHT ON BADGE

Dayton is a senior MI5 officer.

Dan is not surprised and does not move.

> DAYTON (CONT'D)
> I want to show you something.

Dan stares at Dayton for a moment, then saunters over.
Sits down on the sofa, opposite them. Dayton puts his
ID away. Goes to his file. Takes out a PHOTO and slides
it across the coffee table to Dan.

INSERT: TIGHT ON PHOTO

An attractive Chinese woman with long flowing black
hair. Dan looks down at the photo.

> DAYTON (CONT'D)
> Her name was Ling Li—

> DAN
> Yes, I know—

> DAYTON
> She died last week. Massive head
> trauma. The crushing was so bad
> that the top part of her scalp almost
> came off. It's amazing she survived
> this long.

> DAN
> How old was she?

> DAYTON
> Twenty-three.

> DAN
> Twenty-three ... A student?

                    DAYTON
          Well yes, technically.

Dan gives Dayton a quizzical look.

                    DAYTON (CONT'D)
          That's how she got her visa.

                    DAN
          What do you mean?

                    DAYTON
          We think she was posing as a student
          for Chinese Intelligence.

Dan picks up the photo. Looks at it again.

                    DAYTON (CONT'D)
          Part of a Chinese State Security
          undercover cell.

                    DAN
          But you don't know if she was.

                    DAYTON
          We think she was.

                    DAN
          You're not sure though.

                    DAYTON
          Let me say we have reason to believe
          she was. All of this is highly
          confidential, of course.

A pause as Dan puts out his cigarette.

                    DAN
          So why you telling me? I told you
          I can't remember anything.

                    DAYTON
          Because your phone number was written
          on a Post-it note in her room.

                    DAN
          Huh? My number?

                    DAYTON
          The note was torn off, but you could
          see the impression of the number on
          the next page. Look, we don't know
          where she got it or why or when. But
          we've got to ask.

INT. DAN'S FLAT - NIGHT - LATER

Dan sits on the bed facing the window, his back to us.
After a short moment, he goes to the dressing table
and picks up the plastic bag containing his wife's
belongings.

He opens the bag and empties the contents onto the
bed. He picks up the wedding ring and inspects it
closely ... WHEN ...

SOMETHING catches his eye. On the bed, amongst the
belongings.

ANGLE on a small glinting metallic USB stick, about
the size and thickness of a pack of chewing gum.

Dan inspects it carefully, with a confused-thoughtful
gaze. He stands and goes to a small desk, on which
sits a LAPTOP. He inserts the USB stick into the slot
on the laptop.

LAPTOP SCREEN:

'External Hard Drive Found. ENTER PASSWORD' within
a small red window.

Tina Jenkins

Tina Jenkins is a new writer from the South West of England. Tina was accepted onto the MA in Scriptwriting at Bath Spa University in 2009, after being offered a place on the basis of having equivalent life experience to a first class degree. She has a passion for television social dramas, and hopes to forge a career within this area of the industry.

Behind the Truth

Tina has committed to the master's degree whilst in full time employment. Throughout the course she has created some engaging pieces, one of which is the social drama – *Behind the Truth*. Set in the fictional estate of Kingsbury in Bristol, the script tells the story of Neela Mirsha, a fifteen-year-old Pakistani girl, who, out of desperation to conceal her affair with a local bad boy, takes the life of her own brother. As Neela attempts to cope with her guilt, she is faced with a struggle against injustice and an unwanted pregnancy. Ultimately, she is forced to take a stand against all those who seek revenge for the disrespect she has brought upon her family.

Tina would like to take this opportunity to dedicate her part in this anthology in memory of her late father who passed away in 2010.

Behind the Truth

Written by
Tina Jenkins

Tina Jenkins
tina.jenkins1978@mail.com

FADE IN

1. INT: KINGSBURY HIGH SCHOOL — DAY

Teenagers flow out of classrooms into the school
corridor. The air is filled with chatter and laughter,
as groups make their way home. Striking a lonely
figure, NEELA MIRSHA (15), walks up to her school
locker; the word 'paki' is sprayed on its door. She
looks around at all of the white faces and opens the
door. She takes a book out and shuts the locker door.
A Pakistani boy, DEVRAJ MIRSHA (16), is stood behind
the door. NEELA jumps.

                    NEELA
          Dev, you scared me.

                    DEVRAJ
          Racist fuckers!

                    NEELA
          It's fine. The school will clean it
          off again.

                    DEVRAJ
          Bloody right they will.

DEVRAJ puts his hand in his pockets and rummages
around. He hands NEELA some cash.

                    NEELA
          Thought you were walking me
          home!

                    DEVRAJ
          Plans change.

                    NEELA
          Mum'll kill me.

> DEVRAJ
> You'll get over it.

DEVRAJ taps NEELA on the head and walks away. She shuts her locker begrudgingly and traces the graffiti with her finger.

2. EXT: KINGSBURY HIGH SCHOOL — DAY

NEELA walks out into the empty school car park and watches the last of the school buses pull out. She resigns herself to the long walk home and heads for the school gate. STEVE BAKER (17) is leaning out of a car speaking to his friend, JAY PARKMAN (16). They are drinking and smoking a joint. They spot NEELA leaving the school. JAY looks at NEELA and sneers. He passes his can of beer to STEVE and starts to walk over.

> STEVE
> Where you going?

JAY steps up his pace. As NEELA picks up her pace, JAY puts his hand out on her shoulder.

> NEELA
> Go away, would you?

> JAY
> Ouch, that hurt.

NEELA takes his hand off her shoulder and tries to leave, but JAY blocks her exit with his hands.

> JAY (CONT'D)
> I can help. You know, show you about. Teach you English?

He steers her around in the direction of STEVE.

> JAY (CONT'D))
> Come chill out for a bit.

STEVE gets out of the car and makes his way over, as
JAY offers NEELA the joint.

> STEVE
> Get a jog on, mate. I didn't boost
> a car to be stuck watching you try
> to pull.

> JAY
> Mate, I might not have had a shag for
> a while, but I ain't that desperate.

JAY drops his arm and NEELA makes a run for it. STEVE
starts making his way back to the car. JAY runs to
catch up with him.

> STEVE
> Good, thought you were gonna slum it
> there for a sec.

> JAY
> Cheers mate. What do you think I am?

3. EXT: A SUBURBAN STREET — DAY

The rain begins to fall. NEELA makes her way along
the road, past boarded-up shops and spray-painted
walls. She drops her head and makes her way to a high-
rise block of flats. She hears a car slowing its speed
on the road beside her. She quickens her pace, and
makes it into the flats. She presses the lift buttons
— out of order. She heads for the stairs. She hears
footsteps behind her. They quicken, so she quickens.
She begins to get breathless. Suddenly, a hand clamps
down on her shoulder. STEVE turns her round, and pulls
her back down a few steps.

> STEVE
> You can move, you know.

NEELA turns around and tries to move away. STEVE tries
to kiss her, but she rejects him.

>   STEVE (CONT'D)
>   I got a car. Do you wanna go
>   somewhere?

>   NEELA
>   You mean you wanna slum it?

>   STEVE
>   Sorry about that.

STEVE relaxes his grip on NEELA and turns away
from her.

>   STEVE (CONT'D)
>   Fine!

NEELA reaches out her hand to him.

>   NEELA
>   How's your mum?

STEVE turns back to NEELA and embraces her.

>   STEVE
>   Really, don't spoil the
>   mood.

>   NEELA
>   If it was that easy.

>   STEVE
>   Just the two of us.

NEELA and STEVE kiss, but they hear someone coming.

>   STEVE (CONT'D)
>   Meet me in the park later. I'll text
>   you. I love you.

NEELA gives STEVE a quick embrace and rushes off.
STEVE stands there for a moment, frozen to the spot.
Suddenly, his text message alert goes off. The text
appears on screen: 'Luv U 2'. STEVE smiles and pockets
the phone. He rushes down the stairs.

4. INT: THE MIRSHA FLAT — DAY

NEELA opens the door to a small maisonette. It's dark
and pokey. NEELA realises she's home alone. As she
dumps her school bag, she starts to go upstairs, but
BINDIYA MIRSHA (45) enters behind her.

> BINDIYA
> Neela, you're home late.

> NEELA
> I had to walk home. I missed the bus.

BINDIYA kicks off her shoes and hands NEELA
a shopping bag.

> BINDIYA
> You never use your head!

> NEELA
> Sorry Mum.

> BINDIYA
> Just stick the bag in the kitchen.
> I'm already running behind. Where's
> your brother?

> NEELA
> He's gone to Mohan again. I'm sorry.

> BINDIYA
> Such a good boy. You should
> try it.

BINDIYA motions NEELA into the kitchen. NEELA reluctantly takes her mum's shopping into the kitchen.

5. EXT: A DISUSED CAR PARK — DAY

A decrepit car park - the only occupants wander aimlessly with cans of Tennent's Super. An out of place BMW car sits alone, parked in the corner. DEVRAJ enters the car park in his school uniform. He strolls up to the car window. An older, smartly dressed and suave Pakistani man, MOHAN TIWARI (49), gets out of the car. He smiles and greets DEVRAJ like a long-lost son. They embrace.

                    MOHAN
          Good day at school?

                    DEVRAJ
          I've had better.

                    MOHAN
          Problems?

                    DEVRAJ
          I can handle school.

                    MOHAN
          That's what I like to hear.

                    DEVRAJ
          You got some more stuff for me?

                    MOHAN
          In good time. How's your mum?

                    DEVRAJ
          Good thanks. You should drop by.

MOHAN pulls out three packets of pills and a few bags of weed.

                    DEVRAJ
          Same deal as last time?

                    MOHAN
          Same deal. Same cut.

DEVRAJ takes the drugs and puts them into his school
bag. He turns to leave.

                    MOHAN (CONT'D)
          Tell your mum I'll be round for tea
          tomorrow night. And Dev ...

                    DEVRAJ
          Yeah?

                    MOHAN
          Be smart next time. Leave the uniform
          at home.

MOHAN smiles and gets back into his car. DEVRAJ exits
the car park.

6. INT: MIRSHA HOUSE — NEELA'S ROOM - NIGHT

Old classic rave posters adorn the walls. NEELA storms
into the room. She turns up the drum and bass, slips
into her jeans and hoodie, and collapses onto her bed.
Her phone message alert goes off. She reads the message
and smiles. She begins to put on a bit of make-up.
BINDIYA enters the room without knocking.

                    BINDIYA
          Where do you think you're going?

NEELA grabs her coat and her phone.

                    NEELA
          Out.

                    BINDIYA
          It's a school night.

NEELA laughs at BINDIYA.

                    NEELA
          OK.

NEELA gets past her mum. BINDIYA tries to stop her
daughter and grabs her arm. NEELA shoves her mum off.

                    BINDIYA
          Neela. Stop this now.
          What would your father say?

                    NEELA
          Nothing. He's dead.
              (Beat)
          You can't control me!

BINDIYA slaps NEELA across the face. NEELA recoils in
shock and then storms out. BINDIYA rushes into her
room.

7. INT: THE BAKER FLAT — NIGHT

STEVE walks into the living room, and slumps down
on the sofa with a can of beer and a Pot Noodle. He
reaches for the remote and begins to channel surf. The
front door opens and a lot of giggling can be heard.
GLORIA BAKER (48) crashes through the living room door
with a MAN.

                    GLORIA
          Wayhey. Cheeky boy. Hey Stevie.
          This is ... um.

The MAN and GLORIA burst into fits of laughter. STEVE
gets up and grabs the MAN. He opens the door to throw
the MAN out. NEELA is stood there.

EXT: THE BAKER FLAT — NIGHT

STEVE pulls NEELA into the shadows.

> STEVE
> What are you doing here?

> NEELA
> What's going on?

> STEVE
> Nothing!

> NEELA
> You can tell me.

> STEVE
> Right. More crap to deal
> with.

STEVE pulls NEELA into his arms and kisses her
forehead.

> STEVE (CONT'D)
> Just leave Neela!

> NEELA
> No, I wanna ...

> STEVE
> I got it all sorted.

> NEELA
> Please.

> STEVE
> I need to sort stuff here. Stuff you
> don't need to worry about.

STEVE pulls NEELA closer to him and laughs.

> STEVE (CONT'D)
> Everything will be sorted soon.
> I promise.

> NEELA
> I knew I loved you for a reason.

> STEVE
> More than a pretty face. Let's get
> you home.

8. EXT: THE PARK — NIGHT

The stars shine as NEELA and STEVE walk with their
arms around each other. They look like a perfect
couple in love without a worry in the world. Suddenly,
NEELA spots DEVRAJ. She pushes STEVE behind a wall.

> STEVE
> You trying it on?

> NEELA
> It's Dev!

> STEVE
> What the hell's he doing
> here?

> NEELA
> He's looking for me.

> STEVE
> Here? Nah. No way.

STEVE peers around the corner, as JAY walks up to
DEVRAJ. STEVE goes back behind the wall with NEELA.

> STEVE (CONT'D)
> Look, you should go home.

                         NEELA
              What do you mean?

                         STEVE
              Jay's there.

                         NEELA
              Dev won't get hurt, will he?

STEVE peers back around the wall. JAY and DEVRAJ are
talking. STEVE goes back to NEELA.

                         STEVE
              I'll check it out. Just get home.
              I'll text you.

NEELA smiles and sneaks off unseen. STEVE peers around
the corner, just in time to see an exchange of a
package between the two boys. STEVE doesn't like what
he sees as DEVRAJ and JAY hug like long term friends.
They share a laugh and depart. STEVE steps out fully
from behind the wall.

9. INT: MIRSHA HOUSE — NEELA'S ROOM - DAY

NEELA is staring at a photo on her bedside cabinet —
it's NEELA and her dad. A knock at the window makes
NEELA jump. She turns to see STEVE. She rushes over
and lets him in. As STEVE climbs through the window,
NEELA turns away from him.

                         STEVE
              Shit me. It's cold out there.

NEELA fetches something from beside the photo. STEVE
knows she is worried.

                         STEVE (CONT'D)
              What? I told you I'd sort Jay.

NEELA turns to face STEVE, and hands him a positive pregnancy test stick.

>   STEVE (CONT'D)
>   What the fuck? How'd that happen?

NEELA begins to pace the room. STEVE, in shock, falls back on the bed.

>   NEELA
>   Well, if I need to explain that
>   to you, we're in more trouble than
>   I thought.

STEVE gets up and goes to comfort NEELA.

>   NEELA (CONT'D)
>   We're fucked now. They'll send me to
>   Pakistan ... or worse.

>   STEVE
>   Nah, no way. I'll fix this.

STEVE goes to climb back out of the window.

>   NEELA
>   How? Steve?

STEVE disappears from sight. NEELA watches as he goes.

10. EXT: THE MIRSHA HOUSE — NIGHT

MOHAN'S BMW car pulls up to the block of high-rise flats. He exits the car, and makes his way towards the Mirsha maisonette. From his keys, he finds one, and when he reaches the door, he lets himself in.

11. INT: THE MIRSHA HOUSE — DAY — CONT'D

MOHAN routinely slips off his shoes, and places his briefcase neatly away. He makes his way to the kitchen, where BINDIYA is cooking. She embraces him, and he sneaks a bit of the food. She chastises him. He smiles.

                    BINDIYA
          Tough day?

                    MOHAN
          Always is. Thanks for dinner.

                    BINDIYA
          My pleasure. It's the least
          I can do.

                    MOHAN
          Imran would have been proud
          of you and the children.

                    BINDIYA
          Why don't you wash up?

                    MOHAN
          I'm sorry, I didn't mean ...

                    BINDIYA
          It's fine.

                    MOHAN
          He was my best friend ...

BINDIYA turns away from MOHAN, and wipes a tear from her eye. She continues with the cooking.

                    BINDIYA
          Please stop ...

                    MOHAN
          I'll go wash up.

MOHAN takes one last look at BINDIYA before he exits with a smile.

12. INT: THE MIRSHA HOUSE — BATHROOM — NIGHT

NEELA exits her bedroom, and walks towards the
bathroom. She opens the door to find DEVRAJ doing lines
of coke on the window sill.

                    NEELA
               Are you crazy?

DEVRAJ jumps up in shock and knocks the coke
everywhere. He pulls her in and tries to clear
the mess.

                    DEVRAJ
               You stupid bitch!

                    NEELA
               I'm sorry.

NEELA bends down to help DEVRAJ clear up the mess.

Rob Jennings

Born in Sunderland, Rob Jennings initially followed in his father's footsteps welding at the shipyards, before leaving home to work as a dishwasher in Germany. One year later, he was encouraged to attend culinary school, where he trained as a pastry chef. His career took him to Switzerland, Australia, Spain and Germany, working at some of the world's most elite hotels.

Rob's writing career evolved from magazines and newspaper freelance work, both in the UK and mainland Spain. This led him to enter a scriptwriting competition with the BBC, where he was selected as a finalist from over six hundred entrants. As passion became obsession, he enrolled onto the MA in Scriptwriting at Bath Spa University. His work has a defined Northern gritty edge that holds a level of intrigue, menace and wit – a distinct and individual voice.

North of Tarragon
A raw exploration of life up North

Set in a squalid mining village on the outskirts of Sunderland, this dark, comedic drama follows the lives of a pitiful community trapped in a time warp. The pit itself is long gone, work is hard to come by and money is tight – but the family bond remains unbroken.

Northern legend dictates that the father of the household is the breadwinner, the rock, the tyrant and the nemesis – not to be messed with. So with this, we delve into the lives of a tiny segment of the village, and their understanding of paternity. Fuelled by anger, resentment and heartache, the father/son relationship explodes in a surreal and dysfunctional take on extreme parenting.

North of Tarragon

Written by
Rob Jennings

Rob Jennings
elblason@hotmail.com

1. EXT. STREET. DAY.

A manky old bus drives through a grey, faceless town.

2. INT. BUS. DAY.

MRS COATES (60s, uninteresting, plain) rocks
rhythmically. The windows are sweaty with
condensation. She wipes a port hole. The monotonous
tone of the bus bell rings throughout.

MRS COATES' POV FROM THE TRAVELLING BUS

3. EXT. STREET. DAY.

POLIO PETE (50, shackled by calipers) drags his
disabled legs with huge effort. He WD40s the joints.

Through a downstairs window, GOGGSY'S DAD (45, balding
and sickly) climbs onto a kitchen chair.

A dog strains as it tries to pass something massive.

FATHER COCKBURN (an aging Jason King) shakes the
dribbles, zips up, and continues on his journey.

Through an upstairs window, MITSY (40, buxom and
brash) irons in black bra, heaps of steam, she stares
back at Mrs Coates. MITSY starts to unhook her bra.

4. INT. BUS. DAY.

MRS COATES turns her head away - panic.

5. EXT. STREET. DAY.

GOGGSY'S DAD slips on the chair, his legs dangle
suspended from the ceiling. The BUS DRIVER (40, bad
curly perm, face ravaged by acne) slams the brakes on
- the bus skids to a halt.

6. INT. BUS. DAY.

A close-up on GOGGSY'S face (16, glasses, greasy hair,
skeletal). The bus jolts him forward as it slams to
a halt.

7. INT. BUS. DAY.

The BUS DRIVER stares ahead. Firing jets of compressed
air as the doors glide open. No one exits. The bell
continues ringing as his face rages.

8. INT. WORKING MEN'S CLUB. DAY.

The musty old bar echoes with the chapping of bone
dominoes on melamine sticky tables. The door swings
open as BARNSEY (menacing, meathead) and SPUGGY
(waif-like, skinhead), intimidating, stroll in. POLIO
PETE is rocking back from the bar.

> BARNSEY
> Shift.

> POLIO PETE
> (up close) If I had me legs back,
> I'd kick your teeth down your fat
> bastard throat.

BARNSEY eyeballs as the crippled frame shuffles to
his seat.

> BARNSEY
> Ya worth more scrap.

9. INT. BUS. DAY.

An eclectic blend of ages half fill the bus. HUGHSY
(16, cheeky grin) sits, knees annoyingly rocking the
seat in pressing the bell. STOCKA (16, trying to cop a
sneaky peek at the girls. Goggsy (head on overdrive).
CHUBBS (16, podgy, fit to bust) suckles the metal seat
handle as a young boy scoffs crisps.

10. INT. WORKING MEN'S CLUB. DAY.

BARNSEY stands menacing, surveying the bar. SPUGGY
sidles alongside POLIO PETE.

>   SPUGGY
>   Magic.

>   POLIO PETE
>   Eh!

>   SPUGGY
>   Magic, y'know.

>   (Beat)

>   POLIO PETE
>   I'm not f'kin Tommy Cooper.

>   SPUGGY
>   No ... y'know, feelings, in your 'ead
>   - magic feelin's

>   POLIO PETE
>   (staring)
>   Drugs?

>   SPUGGY
>   No man ... you get to see stuff,
>   spastics, stuff us normal folk can't.

PETE looks confused.

>   SPUGGY
>   (arms swaying)
>   Think ... six numbers and
>   a bonus ball.

>   POLIO PETE
>   Fuck off.

BARNSEY looks around the room. He spots LINDA (slim,
hunched shoulders, pretty in bad light) and ALEC
(pouting top lip, dodgy hair) sitting in the corner,
their heads drop.

11. INT. BUS CAB. DAY.

The BUS DRIVER rages, eyes twitching at the woodpecker
hammering of the bell. His white-knuckle driving
swings the bus, swerving erratically.

12. INT. WORKING MEN'S CLUB. DAY.

A head nod indicates ALEC to move over, he complies.
BARNSEY nestles between the two. BARNSEY'S hand
purposefully lays on LINDA'S bare leg. ALEC watches as
the hand circulates and BARNSEY coldly eyes LINDA.

>   ALEC
>   Oh howay Barnsey, ya not going to
>   punch our lass's whiskers, are ya.

>   BARNSEY
>   An' why not?

>   ALEC
>   Well, it's just, we're sort of ...
>   Tryin' for a bairn y'know.

>   BARNSEY
>   And?

>   ALEC
>   Why ... it's like, we've been
>   saving up sort of thing, y'know.
>   Working Saturdays, all day Sunday
>   sometimes, puttin' bits aside to
>   pay for treatment.

>   BARNSEY
>   Treatments that?

                        ALEC
            IVF y'know.

                        BARNSEY
            And?

                        ALEC
            Well, it's a kind of fatherly pride
            bit, offspring sort of thing. Knowin'
            it's yer own and all that ... It's
            just, well, I don't want to go, sort
            of ... stirring your porridge like.

                        BARNSEY
            What's wrong with my porridge then?

                        ALEC
            Oh nowt Barnsey, nowt, smashin'
            porridge I'm sure, but, I want to be
            certain, you know, the bairn's mine.

BARNSEY slams his concrete fist into ALEC'S nuts.

                        BARNSEY
            Fuck all coming out of your Jap's
            eye, bonny lad.

ALEC rolls around on the floor doubled in agony.
BARNSEY turns to LINDA, She looks at ALEC, then
BARNSEY ... Man or Mouse. A side glance at BARNSEY
with a slight pucker smile, hints at her thoughts.

                        BARNSEY
                      (to Linda)
            Congratulations, you've pulled.

13. INT. BUS CAB. DAY.

The ringing has reached mind-snapping level as the
driver slams the brakes on, hurtling pensioners and
children onto the floor.

                    DRIVER
              THAT'S THE LOT.

14. INT. BUS. DAY.

HUGHSY continues the ringing as the snorting
purple-faced DRIVER stomps frantically to the back
of the bus.

                    DRIVER
              Ring - the bell - one more soddin'
              time - and I'll tear your head off -
              you annoying little ...

DRIVER pauses for the appropriate expletive.
MRS COATES is still eagerly mesmerised by the
outside world.

                    MRS COATES
              They're only bairns.

DRIVER'S head turns slowly.

                    DRIVER
              Bairns!

                    MRS COATES
              Yes ... bairns.

                    DRIVER
              Yours?

                    MRS COATES
              Don't be stupid.

                    DRIVER
              I'm not ... stupid.

DRIVER clocks CHUBBS suckling the seat.

                    DRIVER
          HOY, STOP EATING ME F'KIN BUS.

                    MRS COATES
               (turning to face the driver)
          Now that's disgusting.

The DRIVER loses patience with Mrs COATES.

                    DRIVER
          You're disgusting.

Mrs COATES ruffles her coat, she drops her tone.

                    MRS COATES
               (slowly, retaining her composure)
          I'm not standing for this, I'm
          getting off.

                    DRIVER
          That's right Mrs 'I've got a set of
          bollocks tucked up somewhere in here'
          Doubtfire, off you pop.

                    MRS COATES
               (embittered)
          Spotty bastard.

The DRIVER'S arms wave in a gesture of mass
de-embarkation.

                    DRIVER
          That's it, everybody off. And you
          granddad. Faster ... faster. If it
          was a free buffet, you'd beat Linford
          Christie out of the blocks.(To
          Hughsy) What you doing?

                    HUGHSY
          Gettin' off.

                    DRIVER
          Then ... go, go on.

DRIVER goes eye-to-eye as HUGHSY squeezes past.

                    HUGHSY
          My mam says you had a face like a
          pepperoni pizza at school.

The DRIVER recalls life in a hypnotic trance.

                    DRIVER
          I was a medical phenomenon.

                    HUGHSY
          Skull like a battered golf ball.

                    DRIVER
          Nurse said I was a dermatologist's
          wet dream - whatever that meant.

                    HUGHSY
          Couldn't go out at Halloween, head
          like a glowin' turnip.

DRIVER breaks from the trance.

                    DRIVER
          You Yvonne Hughes's bairn?

                    HUGHSY
          Aye.

                    DRIVER
          Why she can talk, took more fingers
          than a party pack of KitKats.

                    HUGHSY
          They still call you Pus the Bus.

                         DRIVER
              It's no wonder your father fucked
              off an' left ya.

HUGHSY stuffs a single finger gesture at the DRIVER.

                         DRIVER
              Why you little ...

The DRIVER races after the boys, leaving CHUBBS in
the wake.

15. EXT. BUS. DAY.

HUGHSY, STOCKA and GOGGSY race off the bus, DRIVER,
fat, frantic and two steps behind.

                         DRIVER
              It's been a long time comin' ...

16. INT. CAR. DAY.

ALEC sits alone, nervous and twitchy. Engine running
and window down. He glances at the two wooden gates
slightly ajar. He peers back as BARNSEY emerges.
He approaches the car and leans over.

                         BARNSEY
              Don't smell too healthy.

                         ALEC
              What's that?

                         BARNSEY
              Your lass - get her sorted.

                         ALEC
              Aye, sure thing Barnsey.

                         BARNSEY
              Anyway, job's a guddun.

A long uncomfortable stare unsettles ALEC.

> BARNSEY
> Well, aren't ya gonna thank
> us then?

> ALEC
> Oh aye, thanks Barnsey, thanks like.

A 'friendly' slap on the face.

> BARNSEY
> Y'welcome bonny lad - anytime.

LINDA emerges from the doorway, fixing her hair in her compact, straightening her blouse. BARNSEY looks and strides edgily away. ALEC jumps out, flings open the passenger door.

> ALEC
> Get in.

> LINDA
> Who you talkin' to?

> ALEC
> Anybody'd think you enjoyed that.

> LINDA
> An' who says no to Barnsey then?

ALEC shoves LINDA into the seat.

> LINDA
> Hey!

ALEC scuttles round to the driver's side.

> ALEC
> Sometimes I wonder what <u>really</u> happens
> when I'm doublin' up on shifts.

>   LINDA
>   What you trying to say?

As the car pulls off they break into a blistering row.
BARNSEY'S eyes follow.

17. EXT. STREET. DAY.

HUGHSY, STOCKA and GOGGSY slow to a walking pace and
stop as they notice an ambulance parked in their
street. CHUBBS flumps up behind.

>   CHUBBS
>   Hey, that driver, he's jus' ...

Silence, as the four boys stare.

18. INT. AMBULANCE CAB. DAY.

CARLOS and STEVO (1970s throwbacks) are chomping on
doorstep butties.

>   SWITCHBOARD
>   Hoy Chuckle brothers, you two finished
>   down hangman's gulch?

>   CARLOS
>   Oh aye, no rush from here pet, this
>   one's going nowhere ... (to Stevo)
>   Stage two, muscular seizure, grey
>   pallor and blueing tongue.

>   STEVO
>   Classic rigor ...

>   CARLOS
>   Work the limbs, ease them in, bit o'
>   gentle pressure. (smug nod)

>   STEVO
>   Maestro ... snug as a bug in a rug.

                    CARLOS
          I said to ya, didn't I, eh, I
          said to ya ... he's a cert for the
          latex compressible slim-fit bin-bag,
          <u>before</u> I even cut 'im down. No bigger
          than five foot two it says on the ...

They both click the 'inverted fingers'.

                    CARLOS
          ... Manual.

                    STEVO
          And you were spot-on. Mind you, 'is
          feet took some gettin' in.

                    CARLOS
          Nit-picker ... Interesting thing
          though, swellin' tongue, always hangs
          to the left. Blue to the right. His
          was hangin' straight out.

                    STEVO
          Thought but, a lovely blue
          an' all. Bit like our lass's new
          scatter cushions.

                    SWITCHBOARD
          Is them the ones from Argos?

                    STEVO
          Aye, 20 per cent off, chuffed to bits
          she was.

                    SWITCHBOARD
          Eeee, she's got a nose like a shit-
          house rat when it comes to bargains
          your Tracy.

STEVO beams, proud as punch.

                    CARLOS
          So, were ya wanting owt
          bonny lass?

                    SWITCHBOARD
          Oh aye, nearly forgot - there's another
          keeler on Ashdown Road. Thought ya
          might like to hoy him in the back as
          well - save you a journey like.

                    CARLOS
          Hey, stroke o' luck there.

                    STEVO
          Howay, let's get a shifty on,
          pick up a couple of scratch cards
          on the way round.

                    CARLOS
          Might pull off the treble.

                    STEVO
          Exactly.

                    CARLOS
          Make a noise ...

19. EXT. STREET. DAY.

The four boys watch as the siren fires up and the
ambulance races off. GOGGSY walks to his gate, he
stops, hesitant. The other boys stand motionless and
watch. He turns for support. Time stands still.

                    HUGHSY
          Take it easy Goggsy.

The other boys stand stationary, faces offering
remorseful support.

Peg Killian

Peg Killian was born and raised in the Midwestern United States, and received a BA at the University of Wisconsin-La Crosse in Art, with a minor in Creative Writing. She then moved to Maine and received an MA in English with a Creative Writing emphasis from the University of Maine. Her thesis was an epic dark fantasy novel entitled *Bloodlines*. She wanted to unite her skills in art and writing into a career in filmmaking, and was thrilled to be accepted onto Bath Spa University's MA Scriptwriting programme. After completing the programme, she returned to the United States to pursue a career writing for film, television and theatre.

Grace

Grace is a play based on the story of Grace Poole, the woman in *Jane Eyre* who spends over a decade shut away with a madwoman in the attic of Thornfield Hall. A close reading of *Jane Eyre* reveals hints of some sort of past connection between Grace and Edward Rochester. Why would anyone ever agree to do the job she does? The play explores the relationships Rochester has with every female at Thornfield as well as their connections to each other. Grace and Jane are not so very different.

GRACE

Written by
Peg Killian

Peg Killian
jupitergal2@msn.com

CAST (ACT I)

GRACE POOL   Late 20s. A plain but not unattractive
              red-haired woman, stout but not fat. She
              is dressed in a plain 1820s dress.

EDWARD ROCHESTER
              Late 20s. He is of average height
              with dark hair and eyes — not handsome,
              but he carries himself with an air of
              suppressed power, like a caged tiger.
              He is dressed as an 1820s gentleman but
              is not prim or reserved.

JOHN   40s. Edward's valet and the
              male caretaker of Thornfield Hall
              (Edward's home).

CARTER   30s. Local surgeon in Edward's confidence.

BERTHA   About 30. Edward's insane wife. Tall,
              tough-looking, slender but sturdy. White
              Creole, with dark wild hair and dark
              eyes. She wears a simple white 1820s
              shift — almost a nightgown.

ACT ONE, Scene 1

              Set, still in darkness, is as follows:
              date is 1820s. The entire centre stage,
              up to down, is taken up by a room. In
              this room there is a fireplace CL with a
              mirror above it, a bed along the wall
              upstage, lamps circa 1820s, and a few
              small pieces of furniture, including
              three chairs and a dresser with a pitcher
              and basin on it. Two of the chairs are
              side by side in front of the fireplace,
              centre stage, and the third chair
              faces them.

*Downstage of the fireplace is a door which
opens to a similar room taking up the
entire left stage — there is no fireplace
in the left-hand room though, and the
lamps are caged. One of the chairs in the
left-hand room is a sort of commode. In
the very centre of the room is a large
chest. JOHN and CARTER stand on either
side of it — they have just brought it
into the room. GRACE, late 20s, stands
DC, with EDWARD, also late 20s, standing
closely behind her — almost intimately.*

*In the central room, downstage right, is
another door leading to the hallway. The
right stage, up to down, is the hallway
and should be narrower than the two
rooms. On the right wall of the hallway
hang portraits and a large mirror toward
the front (downstage).*

*Below the stage, between it and the
audience, there is an indication of a
small wooded area.*

*EDWARD closes the door to the room as the
LIGHTS rise: The centre room is now lit
as though moonlight is coming through an
invisible window in the 'fourth wall,'
and the glow of lamps and the fireplace
are the only real 'sources' of light. The
room they are in is lit the same way only
slightly dimmer, as though the 'window'
is higher and smaller, and there's no
fireplace glow. Everyone looks at the
chest expectantly yet cautiously. EDWARD
opens the chest. BERTHA, who is inside,
stands up suddenly, as if bursting onto
the stage. She looks at EDWARD.*

BERTHA   That was very naughty of you, Edward.

GRACE   You brought her up in there?

EDWARD   I could not risk her being led up —
              I could not risk anyone seeing her.

CARTER   I gave her something to make her sleep,
              but it has worn off too soon.

              *BERTHA points at GRACE and turns
              to EDWARD.*

BERTHA   Is this your whore?

              *GRACE, wide-eyed, looks to EDWARD for an
              explanation. BERTHA climbs out of the
              box, helped by CARTER. She starts to look
              around the room, staying close to the
              walls, and making a soft moaning noise.*

EDWARD   *(to Grace)* She says that of all women
              she sees.

GRACE   Charming.

EDWARD   She has generally behaved better in the
              company of other women, though, than she
              does in mixed company or that of men.
              (to Bertha) Bertha, this is Grace. She is
              here to be your friend and caretaker.

              *BERTHA looks GRACE over lewdly,
              then smiles.*

BERTHA   Let's make a fire.

GRACE   Not now, dear.

              *At this, BERTHA loses interest in GRACE
              and turns back towards the wall, slowly*

walking along it. JOHN moves the trunk to an upstage corner of the room.

GRACE   Do you like books, Bertha? *(low, to Edward)* Can she read at all?

EDWARD Actually, yes. She was quite normal, I understand, as a young child, with the madness developing around twelve or thirteen. The first signs were rare, infrequent fits, and she was still quite normal most of the time for years after that. That is how she and her family managed to conceal her illness from me before our marriage. But if you give her books now, she will destroy them, rip them apart, use the edges of the paper to cut herself, and try to start fires if she can figure out how to get the paper through the lamp cages.

They ALL watch BERTHA for a moment, as she mumbles low to herself and continues her slow walk. EDWARD urges GRACE, JOHN and CARTER to the door, opens it, and follows them through into Grace's room, then shuts and locks the door behind himself. He nods at JOHN and CARTER, who exit the room, then exit UR.

EDWARD I've given the staff instructions that you may keep odd hours, and to let you have free use of the grounds and the kitchen. Of course, you probably won't be able to take many meals with the others until Bertha's schedule is more predictable.

GRACE   Won't they get suspicious at the amount of food I take, to serve both Bertha and myself?

EDWARD   Possibly, so John will also regularly
              bring some food to be kept in your room.
              I've also instructed Leah, the maid, to
              answer if you call for something. In case
              you need something but are unable to
              leave Bertha. They do all think it's odd,
              granted, and may think the same of you,
              no doubt.

              *JOHN enters UR and brings a smaller trunk
              into Grace's room.*

JOHN   Here are her things, Mrs Poole.

EDWARD   Thank you, John. Please take
              Dr Carter home.

              JOHN nods a bow and exits.

EDWARD   As long as we can otherwise show
              a sense of normalcy, suspicions will
              hopefully fade.

GRACE   What have you, or will you, tell your
              servants about us? Your wife is one
              thing, and you say you want her kept
              secret, but many of these people have
              lived in this town long enough to know
              something of me. There will be talk, as
              to why I'm hidden away most of the time.

EDWARD   No one is to know of Bertha, except for
              you, John and Carter. If you have any
              problems with her, you will ring for
              John and he will help you. As to you, I
              have told them that I am hiring you as a
              favour to both you and your brother, as
              we were friends when we were younger.

GRACE   I will do my best, but this is the sort
              of secret that seems doomed to discovery.

And what is my position to be? What have you hired me to do? I won't be down cleaning rooms, and you already have a housekeeper.

EDWARD   Yes, of course, Mrs Fairfax. She is an excellent woman and very kind. She is diligent in the details of the household, but perhaps not so perceptive in other matters, which I find useful under the present circumstances. I have told her that you will work as a seamstress — something to keep you occupied during your long hours here too.

GRACE   And you assume I know how to mend and sew?

EDWARD   (*taken aback*) Don't you?

GRACE   Yes. But again, you see there are potential flaws in your planning. You are taking a lot for granted. And what is your plan for my sanity, Edward? You know I can't be shut away for long without going mad myself.

He leads her back into Bertha's room.

EDWARD   You will have the key to this inner room. That is where Bertha will stay. It is a comfortable room for her. Keep the door shut and locked as often as possible. You are free to leave for short periods throughout the day, but just make sure her room is locked. No one should be able to hear her from the hall.

He points high up above the audience.

EDWARD   As you can see, there is only this high window here. Her bed and dresser have

been bolted down so that she can't drag
them, and the chairs are not high enough.
I don't want anyone seeing her through a
window. And you see there is no fireplace
in here. The room is warmed by the back
of your fireplace. And her lamps are
caged, of course.

GRACE   Seems quite a lonely existence for her,
                with no views, no fire ...

EDWARD   Yes, the madness itself causes
                loneliness, and to keep her safe
                creates more. But you will talk to her,
                and read to her, and eat with her, and
                be her companion.

GRACE   And who will be mine?

                *EDWARD looks guilty at this, and pauses
                before answering.*

EDWARD   I will not be able to spend time up here
                — my presence upsets Bertha. She may
                surprise you as a companion as well —
                sometimes she is very lucid, though she
                sinks unpredictably into this *(indicates
                Bertha)*. But if the solitude gets too
                much for you, make sure she is secure,
                then you can take an hour or two here
                and there to spend among the oth— the
                servants, or to wander the grounds.

                *He walks through the door back into the
                central room and DC to the edge of the
                stage and acts as if he is looking out a
                window there. It is just large enough for
                GRACE to look out as well — it apparently
                is about chest-high for her, and several
                feet tall. He looks down, towards the
                'woods' below the stage.*

EDWARD   See, Grace? You are never very far from
              nature when you need it.

GRACE looks out and regards the 'trees' below.

GRACE   And what of days off? Harry is away at
              school, and I thank you for that, but he
              will have holidays — when am I to see
              him, and my brother?

EDWARD   Bertha can't be alone for a whole day at
              a time, but when Harry is home with your
              brother at the Grimsby Retreat, you can
              spend several hours there on some of the
              days, and John will check on Bertha.

              *EDWARD stops and regards GRACE, who is
              looking out the window sadly. He steps up
              behind her again.*

EDWARD   Get some sleep now, Grace, once you have
              her settled in.

              *EDWARD exits, closing the door to Grace's
              room behind him. GRACE stares at that
              door for a bit, then turns and stares
              at the other. BERTHA is still moving
              slowly around her room, mumbling low to
              herself. GRACE opens Bertha's trunk and
              finds a brush. Carrying this, she unlocks
              Bertha's door and enters, closing it
              behind her. BERTHA is near a lamp, and
              tries to curl her fingers through the cage
              of it, but the openings are too small, so
              she then tries to rattle the cage, but it
              is solid. She tries harder.*

GRACE   Bertha, don't do that.

              *BERTHA ignores GRACE for a few seconds,
              then slowly turns her head to look at*

> *her. BERTHA's head falls back and she*
> *opens her mouth to emit a guffaw. It lasts*
> *for an uncomfortable amount of time, as*
> *if she's laughing at GRACE.*

GRACE   Would you like to get ready for bed?

> *BERTHA looks at the brush, then the bed,*
> *expressionless, then looks back at GRACE*
> *with contempt.*

BERTHA   Whore. Whore.

GRACE   Bertha. My name is Grace. It is not polite
             to call me 'whore.' I am not your servant
             but I am here to help you, care for you
             and be your companion. We may be here,
             together, alone, for a long, long time.

> *At this, GRACE pauses, faltering just a*
> *little, and swallows before continuing.*
> *BERTHA says nothing, though she seems to*
> *be concentrating hard on GRACE.*

GRACE   I know you understand me. I will treat
             you with kindness and respect and you
             will do the same for me.

> *GRACE lets this sink in. She walks to a*
> *chair and sits down.*

GRACE   It cannot be pleasant to be shut up alone
             with no allies. If you will not respect
             me, I will not stay and care for you. You
             would have to go to an institution and be
             among many dangerous and dirty people.

> *BERTHA reacts at the word 'institution.'*
GRACE   Here, you are safe, it is quiet, and I
             will do what I can to find entertainment
             and occupation for you.

BERTHA looks at GRACE with a slight sneer.

BERTHA
I am Edward's wife, but he is so cruel. He has locked me away with his whore.

GRACE
If you say that again, I will leave. Do you understand?

BERTHA's face twitches and she folds her arms, childlike, over her breasts.

BERTHA
You can't leave. You must stay and care for me.

GRACE
(holds out the brush) Let me help you get ready for bed.

She leads BERTHA to a chair, sits her down and begins brushing her hair.

GRACE
Edward married! You can't know what I have given up to do this, to care for the one person who completely dashed my last hopes.

BERTHA
(taunting) Oh — you love him.

GRACE
No, that's not it. It's not that simple.

BERTHA
(enjoying the sensation of having her hair brushed) Ahhhh.

GRACE
You would have beautiful hair, Bertha, if you kept it brushed and smooth.

BERTHA
I am beautiful, just like my mama. That is why Edward married me and not you. Men only marry beautiful women, of course.

GRACE
That's not always true.

BERTHA   It is for rich men. And for a woman
                to get a rich husband, she must be
                beautiful. You love him though. It is
                a shame. Tell me the story, Grace.

                GRACE continues to brush, thinking for
                a bit before she speaks.

GRACE   I don't know the story. I'm still trying
                to figure it out. Why is Edward compelled
                to keep his wife locked in a house full
                of servants who might discover you any
                day, when he could have kept you much more
                easily and secretly in another place? I
                can't explain it. So, why did I choose to
                come here? I hate confinement, restrictions.
                But Edward is paying me very well. I need
                the money and the security for my son.

BERTHA   Your son?

GRACE   Yes, I have a son, Harry.

BERTHA   Where is your husband?

GRACE   *(beat)* My husband is dead.

BERTHA   Where is your son?

GRACE   Edward has sent him to a good school, as
                part of my payment for caring for you.

BERTHA   *(beat)* Why do you call my husband Edward?

                GRACE stops brushing BERTHA's hair.

GRACE   Let me get a cloth to wash your face.

                She goes into her room to exchange the
                brush for a cloth, which she wets in her
                basin. As she does:

BERTHA   Why do you call my husband Edward?

GRACE   *(returning)* I have known him since
                I was a girl. He was a good friend of
                my brother's.

BERTHA   But you are a servant!

GRACE   I'm not. *(washing Bertha's face)*
                My father was the younger son of a
                gentleman, with no inheritance. He
                went into business, opening the inn at
                Millcote, the Grimsby Retreat. About ten
                years ago, Edward met my brother and
                they became friends. Edward is also the
                younger son of a gentleman, and when
                his father and brother were alive, they
                were not kind to him. He was far happier
                playing with my brother Henry.

BERTHA   And you?

GRACE   My mother died when I was small, and
                my father was so busy running the inn,
                that I ran rather wild with Henry, and
                followed him and his friends whenever
                I could.

BERTHA   *(suspicious)* How old is your son?

GRACE   *(pause)* Nine.

                BERTHA guffaws. She grabs the cloth.

GRACE   What did you feel when you met Edward?
                He's someone who — when you are with him,
                you feel so drawn to him — you would do
                anything for him — he can persuade you to
                do things without question.

BERTHA   When I met Edward? I flattered him. He

admired my charms, my accomplishments.
I secured him. He would do anything for
ME — that is how love should be, Grace.

*Pause. BERTHA holds the cloth in front of
her face coquettishly.*

BERTHA   Your son is nine! *(has revelation)* He is
my husband's child! *(guffaws again)*

GRACE   We were fifteen — barely more than children
ourselves. We were not in love. He just
... defies resistance. Edward was always
trying to escape his father's hold. I had
no designs on him, and did not plan what
happened, but once it had ... I thought
Edward might defy his father and marry me,
for his child's sake.

*BERTHA guffaws and stands, putting the
cloth on her head like a bridal veil.*

BERTHA   *(recites)* Duly considering the causes
for which Matrimony was ordained. First,
it was ordained for the procreation of
children, to be brought up in the fear
and nurture of the Lord, and to the
praise of his holy Name. Secondly, it was
ordained for a remedy against sin, and
to avoid fornication; that such persons
as have not the gift of continency might
marry, and keep themselves undefiled
members of Christ's body.

GRACE   Edward's father forbade it — horrible,
overbearing man. And Edward's older
brother was no better. They sent Edward
off to Jamaica, and arranged a marriage
for me here to keep me quiet. And
arranged his marriage to you, for
your money.

BERTHA   *(correcting)* Beauty! *(recites)* Thirdly,
                it was ordained for the mutual society,
                help, and comfort, that the one ought
                to have of the other, both in prosperity
                and adversity.

                *GRACE slowly takes the cloth from
                BERTHA's head, and wipes her own
                face. BERTHA sits on her bed. GRACE
                extinguishes the lamps, then walks to the
                doorway between their rooms. As she opens
                it to leave Bertha's room, BERTHA says:*

BERTHA   Fear and nurture. Fear and nurture.

                *SFX of a horse galloping away outside.
                BERTHA lies down under her covers. GRACE
                hurries into her room and to her 'window'
                to look out.*

GRACE   My god. He is gone.

                *She goes to the doorway between
                their rooms.*

GRACE   He has solved his problems, Bertha. The
                women in his life safely tucked away in
                his attic, as if we were tucked away just
                as neatly in his own mind, stored where
                he does not have to think of us.

BERTHA   *(from her bed, in the dark)* For the
                mutual society, help, and comfort, that
                the one ought to have of the other, both
                in prosperity and adversity. Grace? Let's
                start a fire.

                LIGHTS fade to black.

Lucy Lott

After graduating from UEA with a first class Drama degree, Lucy moved to London to work in public relations. In 2006 Lucy's love of the theatre took her away from writing press releases and up to the Edinburgh Festival to perform her own one-woman show.

Based in Brighton, Lucy regularly travels to London to volunteer with a number of theatres and charities for young people. In December 2011 *The Unlucky Punch*, a script written by Lucy in collaboration with inclusive theatre company Angel Shed, was performed in Islington by a cast of twenty-five 7-16 year-olds.

Grandpa Egg and the Lostgotten

Grandpa Egg and the Lostgotten is a stage play for children, about what happens to stories when we stop telling them. Maude is a little girl who loves telling stories until, sent to stay with her lonely grandpa and afraid that her parents no longer want to listen to her, all of her stories fly away. Under the mysterious gaze of the Egg Collector, Maude and her grandpa embark on a story-making journey to the Lostgotten, where together they must conquer their fears to retrieve Maude's stories. But, what is this place where stories go, and can Grandpa find the courage to finish his story so that Maude can find hers? Incorporating puppetry, poetry and traditional storytelling, Lucy's play takes children on a magical journey exploring life, death and fear, to discover why every person has a story worth listening to.

Grandpa Egg and the Lostgotten

A one-act play for children (aged 6+)
Written by
Lucy Lott

Lucy Lott
lucylott@hotmail.co.uk

CAST

EGG COLLECTOR
        Narrator. Any age. His face and head
        are hairless. His costume is yellow
        and white.

WORDBIRD   Puppet. A huge bird made of paper.

GRANDPA   In his 80s. He uses a walking stick.

MAUDE   8 (and a half). Red hair.

BOY EGG   Puppet. A boy made of egg shells.

SMALL WORDBIRD
        Puppet. A small bird made of egg shells.

STAGING
The stage is simultaneously home to the world of The
Lostgotten and the world of Grandpa's house. The set
of the latter is likely to demand more space than The
Lostgotten, so how the stage/space is divided should
allow for this.

When the action is about to take place at Grandpa's
house, the Egg Collector should direct the audience's
attention towards it, and throughout these scenes
he should be watching the action as if he too were
the audience. When the action takes place in The
Lostgotten, the characters in Grandpa's house may
freeze so as not to draw attention away from The
Lostgotten. Lighting may also be used to highlight
where the action is taking place.

When the Egg Collector appears to be directing the
characters or action in Grandpa's house, or when
objects move between the two worlds, it happens
without Grandpa or Maude being aware.

Scene 1

EGG COLLECTOR walks through the
audience. On his arm sits WORDBIRD.

EGG COLLECTOR Do not be frightened. I know I look
a little odd but I am in fact very
interesting. Let's break the ice, shall
we? A joke, perhaps? Have you heard
the one about the chicken and the egg?
(Beat) Oh, actually, no. That isn't a
joke at all. It's really quite serious,
in a funny kind of way. Like me.

So, the chicken and the egg. Anyone?
Anybody? Hands up. Wiggle those digits.
Chicken? Egg?

(Pause) None, you eggberts! What came
first is ...

The Story.

EGG COLLECTOR has arrived in The
Lostgotten: a mysterious, cave-like
place, filled with magic eggs in every
shape, size and colour. The eggs glow
and hum like electricity.

Welcome readers, listeners, viewers,
watchers, my lovely little story-
gobblers. Welcome to my world. Let
me introduce ... me. I am the Egg
Collector, obviously. And my truest
feathered friend:

WORDBIRD flies onto her perch. She flaps
her wings: a paper feather falls. The
EGG COLLECTOR unfolds it to reveal a
word, cut out of the paper. He holds it
up to the audience to read:

WORDBIRD

Do you like eggs? Little man there? I'd
bet all my fables that you're a boiled
man. And young sir? Hard yolk or soft?
The beautiful woman at your side, mais
oui. Such a radiant complexion. That'll
be the eggs.

Poached, boiled, fried, scrambled,
baked, en cocotte, what? You see, an egg
is none of those things. Not really.

An egg is a beginning. Crack it open and
what trickles out?

Story.

And this is the place where stories come
when someone stops telling them. This is
the place where beginnings wait to be
begun. This place is ... The Lostgotten.

EGG COLLECTOR Got a little lost? Right. You lose
a story. Lost. I get it. Gotten. The
Lostgotten. Get it?

*WORDBIRD flaps her wings: a feather
falls. It reads:*

?

But the eggs I collect are no ordinary
eggs. If you're looking for a story
about those sorts of eggs, I suggest you
leave. Get a fry up.

You see, inside each one of the eggs I
collect, a story sleeps, a play dreams,
a yarn yawns, a tale tires, a fable
farts under the sheets.

*WORDBIRD flaps her wings: a feather
falls. It reads:*

TRUMP

Beg your birdy pardon.

Sometimes a story is a flash of light.

*WORDBIRD flaps her wings: a flash of
light.*

A colour.

*WORDBIRD flaps her wings: coloured
feathers fall.*

A noise.

WORDBIRD flaps her wings: a heartbeat.

A bad smell.

*WORDBIRD flaps her wings: a feather
falls. It reads:*

BELLY BUTTON CHEESE

(Lying) I don't know what you're talking
about. And sometimes a story is a whole
person. Like this.

We follow his gaze to MAUDE.

Meet Maude. She's at the beginning of
her story. She's only eight.

(To the audience) And a half.

EGG COLLECTOR   She can't hear me. She tells everyone
that. Anyone, in fact. Well, anyone that

will listen. But that's part of the problem, you see. Because Maude doesn't think anyone does. Listen, I mean.

For a tiny teller, this Maude can tell some big stories. Listen to this one. It's about a baby, because in Maude's world there's a new baby on the way. The baby is all Maude's mother and father talk about. All. The. Time.

And a baby wouldn't know an egg if it hatched in its nappy. Would it?

We follow his gaze to MAUDE. She is telling her story. She becomes more and more animated.

MAUDE   But the baby did not like his new home. This home had no warm waters. This home did not hum like heartbeats. This home did not wobble when it walked. And this home belonged to someone else.

EGG COLLECTOR *(To MAUDE)* Pause! *(MAUDE freezes.)* She's good isn't she? She loves stories. Like me.

WORDBIRD flaps her wings: a feather falls. It reads:

ME TOO

(To MAUDE) Play!

MAUDE   So, whose home is it? A girl's, that's whose! With blue eyes blinking and red hair blazing and green boots stamping and pink mouth screaming and—

EGG COLLECTOR Stop!

MAUDE freezes.

This is the sad bit. I'm going to
well up. You see, what's about to happen
is this:

*We follow his gaze to MAUDE. MAUDE
clamps her mouth shut and crosses her
arms over her chest.*

Precisely. Nothing. Maude has decided to
stop telling stories. Yes! I know! Look,
it's painful but you have to hear it.

Maude has stopped telling stories
because she thinks everyone has
stopped listening.

EGG COLLECTOR Goodness, look at me, my hard exterior
is cracking. Perhaps we should take our
minds off Maude for a moment. Let me
introduce you to another kind of story.
Like this.

*We follow his gaze to GRANDPA, seated in
an armchair. On a plate on his lap is a
boiled egg, uneaten.*

Meet Grandpa. He's at the end of his
story. He's not eight.

*GRANDPA leans towards the egg. He sniffs
it. He sticks his fingers up his nose,
and then struggles to get them out.*

Grandpa's big old nose can't sniff out
story smells.

*GRANDPA picks up the egg, holds it to
his ear.*

Or pick out story sounds.

*GRANDPA picks up his spoon, brings it
down on the egg. He misses. GRANDPA rubs
his eyes.*

Or make out story lights. Poor Grandpa.
Poor, old ...

*GRANDPA'S tummy rumbles loudly. He
brings his spoon down with force on the
egg. It shatters.*

Broken Grandpa.

GRANDPA looks at the audience. Freezes.

Well, I don't know about you but now
I feel worse. Positively scrambled.
Beaten. Shell-shocked.

*WORDBIRD flaps her wings: a feather
falls. It reads:*

GET ON WITH IT

So, Maude and Grandpa. One at the
beginning of their story, one at the
end. One who will not tell stories
and one who cannot tell stories. Two
different stories? Perhaps.

You see, in the collecting business
there comes a time, not very often, when
there's a chance to get your hands on a
very rare type of story. That needs to
be told. Needs to be heard.

WORDBIRD flies to his lap.

Isn't that right, birdy?

EGG COLLECTOR And when the opportunity is there you
have to do your best to make that story
happen. Like this!

*The EGG COLLECTOR produces a little
suitcase. He pushes it across the floor.
It lands at MAUDE'S feet, she stares at
it blankly.*

(As MUMMY) The baby's coming.

*MAUDE moves her head from side to side
as if listening to her parents:*

MAUDE   Mama, why are you—

EGG COLLECTOR —*(As DADDY)* The baby's coming.

MAUDE   Papa, what have I—

EGG COLLECTOR —*(As MUMMY)* Drive to the car, get the
hospital, pack the Maude, ring the baby.

MAUDE   Mama, I don't under—

EGG COLLECTOR —*(As DADDY)* Tell Grandpa, we're dropping
Maude off.

MAUDE   Papa, why can't I come with you too?

MAUDE freezes.

EGG COLLECTOR Having a baby is very confusing, isn't
it? But, that's another story.
Ask an adult.

You see, sometimes two stories have to
come together to make ...

*WORDBIRD flaps her wings: a feather
falls. It reads:*

OMELETTE?

No. To make another. A new story. A real
story. The rarest story of all. This.

          Scene 2

GRANDPA'S house. Day.

*In his room is a mountain of brown
boxes, packed to bursting with a
lifetime's assortment of objects. The
floor is littered with broken egg shells.*

*There is one window through which we can
see the time of day: day, sunset, moon,
or sunrise.*

*MAUDE stands facing GRANDPA, her
suitcase held against her chest.
He sits in his armchair. They stare
at each other.*

GRANDPA   You don't say much.

MAUDE shakes her head.

Used to be a chatterbox. Always telling
stories. I remember.

MAUDE shakes her head again.

You did. *(Beat)* I think.

GRANDPA'S tummy rumbles. GRANDPA jumps.

There's no need to shout.

*Without speaking, MAUDE tries to explain
that GRANDPA'S tummy is making the
noise: she shakes her head, points to*

her ears, then to GRANDPA'S tummy.

You want me to eat my own ears? How
would I hear anything?

Scene 3

The Lostgotten.

EGG COLLECTOR   I wonder why Maude isn't speaking at all
now? I thought she had come to stay with
Grandpa while the baby is being born.
Nothing to get eggy about, is it tiny
tellers?

Ah, but you see, for Maude it doesn't
feel that way. Maude doesn't know if
she's ever going home. Maude thinks her
parents might never want to listen to
her again. Ever.

*WORDBIRD flaps her wings: a feather
falls. It reads:*

FRIGHTENING

And that's not the worst part. Oh no.
Something's got to happen to all the
stories that Maude has stopped telling.
Stories don't just disappear, remember?

Scene 4

GRANDPA'S house. Day.

GRANDPA   Listen Maude, you're going to have to
say something. I don't know how long
you'll be staying here so—
*MAUDE opens her mouth, but instead of
speaking, we hear her stories tumble
out uncontrollably. GRANDPA and MAUDE*

listen as MAUDE'S stories fly away; loud
at first, then fading to whispers in the
distance. We can make out fragments of
her previous story; different, jumbled.

MAUDE   (voiceover) Not warm. Not someone. Not
               belonged. Heartbeats blinking. Boots
               blazing. Hair screaming. Eyes wobble.
               This home not home. No home.

               MAUDE is shaking. GRANDPA gets out
               of his chair and walks slowly towards
               MAUDE. He puts his shaky hand on
               her mouth.

GRANDPA   You didn't even move your mouth.

MAUDE   That was my stories, I think.
               They've gone.

GRANDPA   Gone?

MAUDE   No one listens to them anyway.

GRANDPA   Gone where?

                        Scene 5

               The Lostgotten.

EGG COLLECTOR Well tiny tellers, we know where stories
               go when someone stops telling them,
               don't we?

               The eggs in The Lostgotten begin to
               glow, the hum gets louder. EGG COLLECTOR
               goes towards WORDBIRD. She is asleep. He
               strokes her.

               You see, before a story begins it is
               invisible, slippery, difficult to eggs-

splain. But it is also full. Of what?
Anyone? This is egg-stremely important.

WORDBIRD flaps her wings: a feather
falls. It reads:

GROAN

It's full of promise, suspense, wonder!
It's just waiting for someone to crack
it open.

WORDBIRD flaps her wings.

EGG COLLECTOR And that someone is ...

WORDBIRD'S wings flap faster, filling
the air with wind. EGG COLLECTOR nearly
falls over.

You. Me. Us.

Shouting over the wind noise.

Storytellers, one and all. Listen.

The wind stops suddenly.

Can you hear it? Of course not. This
story is golden; *about* to be tolden.

WORDBIRD flies up into the air. Beneath
her are three new magic eggs, bright and
beautiful.

They've arrived. Maude's stories.
They're here.

He picks up a magic egg.
What we have here my fellow story-
munchers, what we have here, is this ...

*WORDBIRD flaps her wings: a feather
falls. It reads:*

A BEGINNING

Scene 6

GRANDPA'S room. Day.

GRANDPA   You must have some idea where
               they've gone?

               MAUDE shrugs. GRANDPA impersonates her.

MAUDE   Why do you care? You never tell
               stories anyway.

GRANDPA   Stories can be very tiring when you're
               old. But you, you're only eight.

MAUDE   And a half.

GRANDPA   You're right. Perhaps it's for the best.
               Every story has to end, and there's only
               disappointment when it does.

MAUDE   Not if it's a happy ending.

GRANDPA   Well, not all stories have those.

               *GRANDPA reaches for MAUDE's suitcase,
               but she holds on to it. Gently, GRANDPA
               coaxes it from MAUDE'S grip. MAUDE
               runs over to the window and looks out.
               GRANDPA looks around for somewhere to
               put MAUDE'S suitcase.*

               I doubt you'll find your stories
               out there.

               GRANDPA slides her suitcase across the

*floor as if storing it away. It lands in
The Lostgotten.*

MAUDE   I'm not looking for my stories.

Scene 7

The Lostgotten.

EGG COLLECTOR *(Placing MAUDE'S eggs into her suitcase)*
A storyteller who doesn't care about
finding their stories? Oh dear. This
means getting the story I want will be
harder than I thought.

You see, I need Maude to want her
stories back. Most tiny tellers do.
Otherwise the story I need, the real
one, won't even get told. Perhaps she'll
feel differently if we tell her exactly
where her stories are? Birdy!

*WORDBIRD flies into the air, flapping
her wings above EGG COLLECTOR. A paper
envelope falls. He catches it.*

You are kind.

Knock, knock!

Patrick Poletti

Patrick Poletti (48) is a London-based actor and business consultant who grew up in the Midwest of the United States. About twenty years ago, he left behind an Aerospace Engineering degree and a corporate career in Hong Kong to train as a stage actor in Bristol. He has since performed repeatedly in the West End, and at many of Britain's repertory theatres. He has also made infrequent appearances on screen, usually playing characters best described as Mr, Dr, or Captain Backstory. His writing work includes short comic monologues, business case studies for role plays and television spec scripts for episodes of *Mad Men* and *New Tricks*.

Reset Button

The following excerpt is from the opening of Patrick's short play *Reset Button*. The story centres around Bob; a cynical, grieving father who must confront the deterioration of his job, his marriage and his faith, when Pete arrives back in his life. Pete's family sued Bob over the car accident that killed his only son and injured Pete. In the final scene, Bob gets a concession from his Bible-fixated wife. He regains his faith and secures a future without reliance on hyper-literate Corporate Policy and the Bible.

RESET BUTTON

Written by
Patrick Poletti

Patrick Poletti
www.patrickpoletti.com

Scene 1

*Present day. A store in a strip mall —
a suburban Chicago branch of the TV and
audio system company, 'Acoustic Visuals'
aka AV.*

*The store's entrance is upstage Centre .
The back and left walls are black tinted
glass with decals facing the unseen
street and sidewalk. They advertise
'Instalment Plans' and 'Installation
Available' but read backwards in the
store. Upstage right is a counter with
two Point of Sale (POS) terminals which
face towards the back. Credit Card
advertisements surround the terminals.*

*The main area of the stage is the store's
demonstration area, which has small sofas
and/or chair set, for experiencing the
(off-stage) products. The onstage POV for
the demo systems are the left side stage
and out front. The front right side of
the stage has a door to the wings, which
represent the store's backroom.*

*Bob Harvey, 52, bearish and tall, even
though he doesn't stand up straight,
passes through the front door. Bob wears
a tweed blazer over khaki slacks and
a faded navy blue button-down shirt.
Surprised that the door is open he
returns his keys to a clip on his belt.*

*Dexter Reid, 35, short, wearing the same
khakis and a brand new navy blue button-
down shirt, fold marks and all, enters
from the backroom going towards the POS
area with a stack of small boxes*

BOB   Didn't know you'd be starting already.

DEXTER   Can you grab a couple of these?

BOB   *(taking three of the small boxes)* Not
               used to anyone here so early.

DEXTER   Thought you start at 8.30?

BOB   I always get here this early.

               *DEXTER and BOB open the boxes, DEXTER
               stacks the contents without looking.
               BOB inspects one of the DVD envelopes.*

BOB   Set-up instructions on DVD?

DEXTER   Corporate made 'em, after those
               consultant reports.

BOB   How are they gonna watch it if they can't
               set up their new system?

DEXTER   Well, they are free.

BOB   *(BOB goes slowly towards the store room
               door)* I wouldn't mind a Consultant's
               salary for asking stupid people
               questions.

DEXTER   That's no way to talk about potential
               customers.

BOB   *(off)* I meant our guys at Corporate.

               *DEXTER ignores the remark and consults
               a clip board as he aligns small Perspex
               signs on the POS counter. BOB returns
               onstage in his faded but perfectly
               ironed, starched AV shirt.*

BOB   (*surveys the store, looking into the
               wings*) I usually straighten, power up the
               units, start the screens running, listen
               for anything out of phase, then I make
               sure ... (*BOB stops himself from further
               instruction*) ... but it's your ship now,
               so ... ?

DEXTER   Nope. Stick to that. Great. (*BOB starts
               towards his routine*) First up though,
               I need you to check this out. We'll be
               running demos with these now.

               *From another box DEXTER unwraps a set of
               video-game controllers. DEXTER points
               the controller towards the wings, starts
               the Star Wars theme and stops it in an
               instant. Bob takes the controller and
               slowly paces around the demo area looking
               at it.*

DEXTER   Who set that *Star Wars* demo music?

BOB   I did. (*BOB points the controller, hits
               a button, nothing happens*)

DEXTER   We shouldn't be using that music without
               written permission.

BOB   What've you got against Star Wars?

DEXTER   One. It's out of date.

BOB   It's immortal. How could it be
               outta date?

DEXTER   Two. Not enough sub-woofer. It's written
               in the Guidance Notes on store acoustics.
               We're s'posed to use *Independence Day*—

BOB   That movie?

DEXTER   —for full sub-woofer experience.

BOB   Wooden stars and CGI is not a movie.
                Star Wars is a movie. Not to mention the
                music. Nobody can hum the *Independence
                Day* theme!

DEXTER   That's what's down in the notes.

BOB   What about the K4s? You don't want a
                sub-woofer with those speakers.

DEXTER   Corporate tracks our add-ons.

BOB   K4s have plenty of boom.

DEXTER   Why wouldn't we want them to buy a sub?

BOB   Because their house will shake so much
                the plasterboard will turn to dust.
                We gonna start writing Home Insurance
                policies now?

DEXTER   That's very cynical. I hope you've
                read Chuck Johnson's Mission Statement.
                Positive Intent is one of the AV Core
                Values. *(refers to the controller)* It's F1
                and square to start, X to stop, triangle
                for settings, except menu which is circle,
                but you have to hold F2, of course.

BOB   Of course. *(tentatively tries some more
                buttons)* Must be muted.

                *BOB stares at the device, presses another
                combination. Lights from an off-stage
                screen shine. Pressing more buttons,
                there's a brief sound of dialogue in
                Chinese, then sound and light stop with
                digital shriek.*

DEXTER   Have a look at the Guidance Notes on Game
                Controllers. The paperwork's in the back.
                (beat) I need you to change into a new
                shirt. That one makes you look ...
                (gestures) Yours has faded, so ...

BOB   Uh, yeah, sure.

                *BOB grumbles and slowly goes towards the
                store room.*

DEXTER   Saw that Coffee-Mania on the corner,
                I thought I'd grab some fuel before we
                open. Bring ya back something?

BOB   *(exiting into the store room)* All set.
                Thanks.

                *DEXTER starts to leave as MAGGIE enters
                the store's front door. She is in her
                early forties, short and a little plump.
                She wears jeans and, over a white
                turtleneck, a sweatshirt with a knitted
                WWJD pattern. She carries two stainless
                coffee mugs and a brown paper bag.*

DEXTER   Sorry ma'am, we open in about an hour.

MAGGIE   Hour and a half. *(beat)* I'm Bob's wife
                Maggie.

DEXTER   Dexter. Dexter Reid. *(the name means
                nothing to MAGGIE)* The new manager?

MAGGIE   Oh.

DEXTER   You work in radio.

MAGGIE   *(still registering DEXTER as the new
                manager)* What radio?

BOB   What kinda music do they play? Or is WWJD
                 news and talk?

MAGGIE   No it's an expression. *(steps away from
                 him)* When did you start?

DEXTER   Took weeks to get the paperwork
                 together, only started today. What's
                 the expression?

MAGGIE   What Would Jesus Do?

DEXTER   Oh. Of course. *(holds his hands up
                 apologetically)* Religious questions in
                 the workplace. Can't really engage.
                 Sorry.

MAGGIE   Yes. So you've known for a couple weeks.
                 Congratulations.

DEXTER   Yeah, cool huh? *(points to her mugs)* I'm
                 headed across the street but I see you've
                 got one already. Maybe I'll see ya later.
                 Bob! Hurry up.

                 *DEXTER exits. MAGGIE drinks from her own
                 mug, places the second mug and paper bag
                 on the POS counter. Maggie briefly looks
                 to the ceiling, closes her eyes and
                 takes a deep calming breath. BOB begins
                 speaking just before he enters.*

BOB   *(tucking in his new shirt, with its
                 visible fold marks)* Calm down Dex ...

MAGGIE   Not much chance of that. *(a long silent
                 stare at Bob)*

BOB   How long have you been here?

MAGGIE   Only long enough to meet the new manager.

BOB   Ah. *(pause)*

MAGGIE   That shirt looks terrible, what happened
             to the one I ironed?

BOB   Faded. At least I think that's what
             he meant.

MAGGIE   And when did you plan on telling me?

BOB   Just didn't come up. I was gonna wait
             'til he started for sure. It's only his
             first day.

MAGGIE   You've known it Bob, and you haven't
             told me. It's a lie by any Scriptural
             definition.

BOB   You're right.

MAGGIE   I forgive you. *(BOB takes a stainless
             cup and looks with anticipation in the
             paper bag)* Thanks. Love it when you make
             me these.

MAGGIE   It was a double batch for the Mission
             Centre, thought you'd like the rejects.

BOB   *(sniffing the bag)* Huh?

MAGGIE   I hate it when they're not symmetrical.
             (pause) Now who's Dexter?

BOB   *(biting into a muffin)* Used to be at
             a downtown mall.

MAGGIE   Downtown? I knew he smelled of alcohol.

BOB   Maggie ... *(eats more)* Turns out, having
             my own store didn't count for much in the
             recruitment report, so technically, I

didn't meet all the competency points
for the job—

MAGGIE   It's a test, Bob, nothing more. We're
                fine. God has a plan and this is just
                another test.

BOB   We have had our test.

MAGGIE   I don't wanna hear it.

BOB   *(eating)* Lucky Mission Centre. Dunno
                why we're feeding people, we're the
                ones broke.

MAGGIE   Bob, I'm proud to be there. *(a relieving
                smile)* That church is firmly rooted in
                Scripture.

BOB   Roots ... ? They got a place for us when
                the bank takes the house?

MAGGIE   That was just the first notice. We've
                got plenty of time. The Lord works in
                wondrous ways—

BOB   He's running out of time. That was the
                first in writing, they've been calling me
                for three months.

MAGGIE   They are getting something from us
                every month.

BOB   It's nowhere near the full amount.

MAGGIE   It's better than most of their customers.
                I doubt we're first on their list. *(an
                uncomfortable silence)* A prayer before
                you start your day?

                MAGGIE reaches to grab his hand, BOB

makes one step away from her and continues eating.

BOB   Not now Maggie.

MAGGIE   You used to always ... *(he turns further away sipping coffee. She prays by herself, wrists and hands open upwards)* Lord, we just want—

BOB   Not now.

MAGGIE doesn't stop, continues mumbling. BOB puts down his food, picks up a game controller. He hums the Star Wars music, presses buttons but nothing happens. Maggie hands widen. Bob presses more buttons. Suddenly lights shine from out front. The sound of a crowd clapping. The television evangelist preacher Joel Osteen is heard saying 'All right, hold up your Bibles, join me friends, and repeat after me.'

MAGGIE   *(turns towards the light)* Oh I love these two.

BOB tries to turn off the religious television show. Nothing happens. He keeps trying. The preacher continues 'Stand with your arms raised. This is my Bible.'

MAGGIE   *(Her right arm is above her head palm forward. She speaks in unison with the TV preacher and his bleating congregation.)*'I am what it says I am, I have what it says I have, I can do what it says I can do. Today I will be taught the word of God—'

BOB smashes the controller into the floor.
The religious broadcast stops.

BOB   That's enough of that.

MAGGIE   'A day hemmed with prayer is less likely
               to unravel.'

BOB   Sorry. I didn't sleep well.

MAGGIE   That doesn't forgive anything. *(pause)*
               Same dream?

BOB   Different again. He was on his bike, very
               young then, I'd just removed his training
               wheels. He was doing great, then a phone
               rang, and I was back in the kitchen, the
               same police officer on the phone, but
               there was a crackle on the line ... I
               kept asking are they OK? Are they OK?
               'You'll have to read the report sir, the
               car's totalled, I'll have to fax you the
               report' and I woke up.

MAGGIE   Bob, God is waiting to help us through
               it. To reveal his plan for our lives.

               BOB attempts to put the controller back
               together. The repair falls apart as he
               puts it back onto the counter.

BOB   *(BOB walks away from MAGGIE)* When are
               you gonna learn? Torment. Part of His
               Plan? It's not user friendly. I doubt the
               Guidance Notes too.

MAGGIE   I don't want to hear it. *(pause)*

BOB   He's short-changed us. I got to work on
               the bank not God. When they find out I'm
               on wages, they're gonna move on us quick.

MAGGIE   God hasn't abandoned you. I'm speaking
                to Pastor and Virginia about some
                counselling.

BOB   I'm not sitting down with Ray and Ginny
                to discuss accepting God's will. Those
                people telling us how to behave?

MAGGIE   You been lost since Jimmy was taken from
                us. I've been able to anchor myself
                there, they could—

BOB   They don't know loss. What could
                they say? Just repeat verses until they
                get a smile out of us. He never had to
                make payroll.

MAGGIE   You're crabby 'cause you've not had any
                sleep. If you'd get back to your prayers
                — you'll see.

BOB   I'll see. I'll see the guy from
                the bank saying 'Hi' *(gestures)* on
                a Sunday morning and locking us out
                of our house Monday.

MAGGIE   God has a path for us Bob.

BOB   Then you better stay on yours. Go ahead.
                Get over to the Mission Centre. I'll
                figure out what to say to the bank.

                MAGGIE stares at Bob then exits. BOB
                takes another big bite of the muffin. He
                drinks his coffee while he straightens
                items on the shop floor.

                The front door opens and Pete enters.
                He is 23, tall, collegiate, but with a
                slight limp and a scar on his forehead.
                He wears a light jacket over a shirt

that's the same as BOB's AV uniform.

BOB   We don't open 'til nine. *(recognising Pete)* What in the hell are you doing in here?

PETE   I tried to get a hold of you before—

BOB   Get outta here.

PETE   The restraining order's expired, you won't be in any trouble. Where's Dexter?

BOB   You know Dexter?

PETE   He hired me as a Team Member.

BOB   Is this your idea of a sick joke?

PETE   Of course not Mr Harvey. I requested to be back in my hometown.

BOB   What?

PETE   I applied through Corporate's Federal job programme. Only found out yesterday you worked here.

BOB   Pete, this—

PETE   As soon as I heard I knew this was exactly what was supposed to happen.

BOB   Please don't mention God's plan.

Shannon Tweed

Shannon Tweed was born in Northern Ireland in 1987. She attended the University of Dundee in 2005 where she studied an English Literature and American Studies MA (Hons). She enrolled on this MA programme to learn the principles behind scriptwriting in the hopes of broadening her writing abilities. Over the programme she has written a gothic theatre play and two films, both coming of age dramas that are based in the off-the-wall and fantasy genres..

Bright-Line

Bright-Line is a surrealist drama with noir undertones. It is the story of Lucy Jones, a young woman who has been finding mysteries her entire life where there are none, until she comes across a dead clown in her isolated island town. The visiting circus say they aren't missing any performers. As this clown is revealed to be her long-lost uncle, Lucy mounts an investigation into why he would return to a town he was disgraced in. Through her search she forms a romantic attachment to the troubled ringmaster, Gaston, and uncovers a series of unspoken problems within her family and her claustrophobic community.

BRIGHT-LINE

Written by
Shannon Tweed

Shannon Tweed
shannon.tweed@bathspa.org

FADE IN.

1. EXT. THE SEA. PASSENGER FERRY. DAY.

A dazzlingly sunny day. Sea wakes play against
the sides of a ferry. A brightly coloured, busy,
travelling circus on the open car deck. A few
'ordinary' cars and beige passengers are dotted
around the circus caravans and jeeps.

In the midst of the circus sits an old-fashioned
wooden wagon, tied to a tow. *Circus Vegas* is painted
across its flank.

Most of the circus folk, in their full costumes and
make-up, are outside their vehicles enjoying the air
or smoking. The other passengers remain inside their
white family cars with the windows up.

A MIME spots a little GIRL in the backseat of a family
car staring in awe at the circus.

The MIME plucks a pink helium balloon from a bundle
and taps the GIRL's window. The GIRL tries the window
and then the door, but they are child-locked. She
looks askance at her parents but they turn up their
conservative music, staring ahead.

The MIME lets the balloon go and we follow its
progress as it travels upwards.

                                        CONT.

2. EXT. THE SEA. JAMESTOWN. DAY.

The ferry is headed towards a small island isolated in
the sea, JAMESTOWN. The healthy balloon floats towards
the sky.

                    LUCY
                  (V.O.)
            What is love? Is it truth or loyalty?
            Family or friend?

A breeze redirects the balloon's course. It travels over a wholesome suburbia.

The power line, towards which the balloon is being buffered, is revealed.

> LUCY (CONT'D)
> Here in Jamestown, blood is thicker than water. And we never understand when our beloved turn away. Yet sometimes, when we do leave, we leave a little something behind. Unfinished.

The balloon grows increasingly closer to the power line.

> LUCY (CONT'D)
> I think that's why the events that broke our town hurt me so personally. Because I also loved our town.
> (Pause.)
> But at 8.30pm, on a slow Saturday evening, a man tried to walk from one end of Jamestown to the other ...

The balloon hits a power line and explodes, fragments falling through the air.

> LUCY (CONT'D)
> ... and did not succeed.

> CUT TO:

3. EXT. JAMESTOWN. DAY.

A battered old Fiat pulls up outside *Jamestown Glassware*.

> CONT.

4. INT. JAMESTOWN. RICH'S CAR. DAY.

Inside the car, the driver is dressed in full clown

regalia. He pulls a red nose from his pocket. His
inexperience shows as he has trouble working out how
to put it on.

An incubator is strapped in on the passenger seat, and
plugged into the cigarette lighter. The CLOWN removes
his sunglasses and turns off the ignition. The light on
the incubator flicks off.

The CLOWN puts his hand to the incubator heater, then
fumbles in the hay inside of it, and extracts three
unusual eggs. He looks around for a place to put them,
checking the glove compartment and then his watch.

He sees someone through the windscreen (O.S.) He
kisses his fingers in that person's direction then
pauses.

He panics because there has been no response - that
person hasn't seen his gesture.

He almost drops an egg. He grabs at it like it's very
precious, and mops his brow when it's secure in his
hand again. He gets out of the car.

                                        CUT TO:

5. EXT. LUCY'S STREET. THAT AFTERNOON.

Neighbours roll out spanking clean bins to their
pavements.
                                        CONT.

6. EXT. LUCY'S HOUSE. AFTERNOON.

A white-washed, well-kept house. sunny autumn day.
(O.S.) A television blares.
                                        CONT.

7. INT. LUCY'S HOUSE. AFTERNOON.

LUCY's small room is a melody of neat and ordered.
A mannequin is only garment on it is LUCY's
Neighbourhood Watch 'Captain' sash and badge.

A large photo of a young man (23) sits on her vanity
table, his arm around a seven year old LUCY. They
grin.
A small television shows a clean cut detective
effortlessly arresting a bad criminal.

A giant Rubik's Cube dominates the bedroom. It is
comprised of hundreds of individual, completed Rubik's
Cubes and is nearly complete.

LUCY JONES (21) big blonde hair, full makeup,
conservative but fashionable dress except for a pair
of contrasting white sports trainers. LUCY applies
glue to a Rubik's Cube.

                    LUCY
            (In unison with the TV detective.)
          These here, are my streets.

Lucy looks at her watch. She lifts the sash off the
mannequin, accidently knocking the photograph as she
turns off her television as it issues a gunshot sound
effect.

She gently puts the photograph to rights.

                        CUT TO FLASHBACK:

TITLE CARD: WHEN EVERYONE KNEW WHERE THEY WERE.

8. EXT. A JAMESTOWN FIELD. DAY.

RICH JONES (23) thin and fidgety, and LUCY (7) straddle
bicycles at the side of the empty field, leaning over
their handlebars.

                    RICH
          Ready shortarse?

LUCY puts a foot on her peddle.

                    RICH (CONT'D)
          One, two, two and three quarters—

                    LUCY
          Riiiccch!

                    RICH
          GO!

LUCY pelts forward, awkward but determined. RICH
pretends to start but he's letting her win. As the
'race' progresses, RICH tails her and woohoos loudly.

LUCY skids on a pebble. Her bike veers wildly towards
the embankment that leads down to a road.

                    RICH (CONT'D)
          Shit.

RICH picks up speed and kicks LUCY's bike out from
under her to stop her from going over the edge into an
oncoming car. LUCY falls to the ground.

RICH helps her up.

                    RICH (CONT'D)
          You all right?

                    LUCY
          Yeah.

                    RICH
               (Joking.)
          Don't tell Rita until I'm safely in
          Alaska, OK?

LUCY manages a smile.

                              END FLASHBACK. CUT TO:

9. EXT. GARFIELD STREET. EARLY EVENING.

LUCY, wearing her sash, stands in the middle of the
street beside two other Neighbourhood Watch members.
GEORGE (40) a tastefully dressed transvestite, and
ALEX (16, female) black pigtails and a lip ring. All
three stare intently up at -

A large ball of yellow and red wool caught in the high
branches of an oak tree. An unravelled thread of the
wool blows in the breeze.

A BOY (8) jiggles from foot to foot beside them.

                    BOY
          And I kicked it like this, and then
          it went way up in the air, but I
          tried to catch it before it got up
          there and got stuck, but then -

LUCY pats the BOY'S shoulder.

                    LUCY
          It's OK, hun. You let us deal with
          it now.

                    GEORGE
          I-I could climb up there?

LUCY raises her hand in a stop gesture.

                    LUCY
          Too dangerous, George. There's every
          chance you might fall.

A couple cut across the street between the tree and
the Neighbourhood Watch team.

> LUCY (CONT'D)
> (Under her breath.)
> Newcomers.

GEORGE nods sagely. ALEX rolls her head back for an exasperated moment.

> ALEX
> Yeah - I need to get home sometime this year, Lucy. It's like Batman-o'clock.

LUCY registers that a group of neighbours have formed an audience on the pavement, some with dogs or children.

Behind them, she glimpses a clown figure further down the street. He is obscured by the crowd and the shadows, but he waves at LUCY, then signals for her to join him around the corner, before going in that direction himself.

> GEORGE
> Well Lucy, what's the plan of action?

LUCY returns her attention to the situation. She walks to the tree and pulls a black cat off its trunk. The animal swipes at the loose wool thread.

> GEORGE (CONT'D)
> That's it, I'm ringing Leona.

> LUCY
> That won't be necessary.

ALEX sighs pointedly.

> LUCY (CONT'D)
> Anyone happen to see a stick?

All three look around like the three stooges. After a moment, the group of neighbours follow suit.

A police car appears at the bottom of the road.

> GEORGE
> Lucy ...

LUCY sighs.

> LUCY
> Look more quickly.

CUT TO:

10. EXT. GARFIELD STREET. EARLY EVENING.

A police car sits under the tree, door open. A smug
POLICEMAN hands a riled LUCY the ball of wool.

> POLICEMAN
> Mind the loose bit now.

CUT TO:

11. EXT. GARFIELD STREET. A SUBURBAN HOUSE.
AN HOUR LATER.

LUCY leans on her leg to pen a smiley face on a
leaflet. It reads: 'Save Our Neighbourhood Watch -
Protecting Your Streets Over the Last 4 Months!'
Underneath, cartoons of thieves and knife-wielders
behind bars.

LUCY slips the leaflet through the letter box in
the front door. Below it sit three empty milk jars;
a five-pound note slipped underneath the jars - the
milk money.

LUCY folds a second leaflet, lifting a jar to place
it underneath, the money takes off in the wind.
At this moment the HOUSE OWNER appears at the door
to witness this.

LUCY looks back at him nervously.

                                              CUT TO:

12. INT. JONES' BISTRO. LATER THAT EVENING.

A traditional bistro, plastic plants and decorated in
rich colours.

LUCY makes her way to the bar where KARL (40) handsome
and small town suave, stands joking with a couple
of off-duty policemen. He puts his arm around LUCY's
shoulders, then signals her sash.

                    KARL
          They paying you for this yet?

                    LUCY
          Nope.

KARL disengages his arm to begin a large drinks order.

                    KARL
          Let me tell you something. The best
          thanks comes in the form of a crisp
          twenty-pound note. OK?

                    LUCY
          Uh-huh.

RITA (40) graceful and seductive, playfully whips KARL
with a tea towel.

                    RITA
          Leave her be.

                    KARL
          I can't ask a question anymore?

                    RITA
          No.

                    LUCY
          Anyway, I'm only passing through for
          some water.

KARL claps his hands at the BARTENDER.

                    KARL
          I need a glass of the finest water our
          prehistoric pipes can trickle out.

KARL takes the water and hands it to LUCY.

                    LUCY
          Thanks.

CHIEF INSPECTOR DUNN (60) portly with a bulldog
expression, enters the bistro with GARY (76) a broken
man. The bistro hushes until DUNN pointedly places a
hand on GARY's shoulder.

RITA smiles at DUNN as he makes his way to the bar. He
kisses RITA's cheek and takes a bar stool. KARL nods
at DUNN.
                    LUCY (CONT'D)
          Who's that?

                    DUNN
          Gary? You wouldn't know him. Gent's
          been in prison for the last 24 years.

                    LUCY
          What for?

                    DUNN
          Charged with his wife's murder.

LUCY begins to shake her head.

                    KARL
          Rita said he's innocent?

> DUNN
> Oh yeah. Turns out he decided someone
> was trying to poison her, so he
> starts digging around, gets his hands
> dirty. Then she's found dead, and he
> hasn't been in work that day.
> No alibi.

> LUCY
> So where had he been?

> DUNN
> 'Spying'.

DUNN takes a swig of his drink. Then points at
LUCY's sash.

> DUNN (CONT'D)
> Just goes to show, Lucy - always
> leave the investigation stuff up to
> yours truly.

LUCY looks over at GARY. The YOUNG FAMILY he has
been sitting next to get up and leave. He examines a
painting, looks around hopefully, then fidgets with a
sugar packet.

> DUNN (CONT'D)
> How's about a tune for the oldies?

KARL presses the play button on the ancient stereo,
tinny music fills the bistro. KARL tosses LUCY a cloth.

> KARL
> (To Lucy.)
> Make yourself useful.

> LUCY
> Sorry, it's my night off.

> KARL
> I know a dozen people that would kill
> to wipe my tables.

> LUCY
> Well you know, nothing says thank you
> like a crisp twenty.

KARL arranges the many drinks on a tray.

> KARL
> Yeah, yeah. Lucy please, the
> bin bags, I beg of you. Just the
> bin bags.

LUCY rolls her eyes.

> CUT TO:

13. INT. THE BISTRO. THE BACK HALLWAY. THAT EVENING.

Two bin bags sit outside the toilet door. (O.S.) The
toilet flushes.

LUCY opens the door and picks up the bin bags, taking
them down the hall.

> CONT.

14. EXT. ALLEYWAY BEHIND THE BISTRO. THAT EVENING.

An alleyway with industrial bins. An overhead light
is malfunctioning and flickers on and off, flooding
the alley with light and plunging it into complete
blackness in quick succession.

The CLOWN struggles limply inside the bin, his arms
draped over the edge. A deflated Jack-in-the-Box in the
flickering light.

LUCY drops the bin bags.

C.U. THE CLOWN'S EYES, IRISES ROLLING.

> LUCY
> Sir? Have you been drinking?

C.U. A LINE OF BLOOD SEEPS DOWN FROM BOTH EDGES OF THE
CLOWN'S MOUTH ONTO HIS CONVULSING CHIN.

> LUCY (CONT'D)
> Wait there. I'll get help.

(O.S.) A bottle is disturbed near her in the alleyway.
She turns her attention towards it, moving forwards.

The CLOWN whimpers loudly and LUCY responds to
this first.

> LUCY (CONT'D)
> It's going to be all right.

LUCY now makes her way to the bin. Her hand makes
contact with the CLOWN's lapels. The CLOWN grasps
LUCY's hand with difficulty. After several attempts he
manages to gurgle the word 'Eagle' —

Suddenly, a figure takes LUCY in a headlock from
behind. She struggles to turn. He brings a gun to
her head.

She is kicked against the wall, and knocked semi-
conscious. From the ground, LUCY hears smashing glass
and retreating footsteps.

> CUT TO:

15. EXT. CIRCUS ALLOTMENT. LATER THAT EVENING.

A rusting sign on a wooden fence says
'No Trespassers'. White circus tents of various
shapes and sizes surround a huge central tent.
Rain batters down on the grass. Mud climbs up the

bottom flaps of the white tents. The wooden wagon's
wheels sink into the sludge. The pick and chain
securing it to the earth are loosening slightly.

                    GASTON
               (O.S. Into phone)
          I did turn right ... I did.

GASTON LA SALLE (30) comes into shot. He is built like
a lumberjack and wears a sequined ringmaster's costume
complete with eyeliner. He shields his head from the
worst of the rain with a plastic yellow cowboy hat.
A mobile phone is pressed to his ear.

Hannah Willcock

Hannah Willcock was born in Cornwall, and studied at University College Plymouth St Mark and St John, where she graduated with a first class honours degree in Creative Writing with English Language and Linguistics in 2010. In order to explore her passion for scriptwriting, she enrolled on the MA programme at Bath Spa University, where she developed a variety of original work, including two plays for radio and a ninety-minute film script for television.

Postman's Knock

Hannah has a keen interest in contemporary, domestic drama, and particularly enjoys writing stories about extraordinary emotions experienced by people leading seemingly ordinary lives. One of these stories is *Postman's Knock*. Written as a single drama for television, the script tells the story of Pete Thompson, a postman whose obsession with time prevents him from having personal relationships. On discovering that his ex-girlfriend Samantha has become engaged to a con man, Pete vows to do all he can to expose Sam's fiancé as a fraud. In order to succeed, he requires the help of Royal Mail customer, Inez, a seemingly frail and isolated woman, with whom Pete believes he has little in common. However, Inez has other ideas, and is soon manipulating Pete for her own agenda – finding her long-lost son.

POSTMAN'S KNOCK

by
Hannah Willcock

Hannah Willcock
hannahwillcock@yahoo.co.uk

1. INT. PETE'S FLAT, KITCHEN - EARLY MORNING

CLOSE-UP: A MALE HAND PICKS UP AN EGG-TIMER FROM A
KITCHEN WORKTOP. THE HAND FREEZES MID-AIR.

PULL BACK: PETE, 30, clean shaven, with short dark
hair, wearing a freshly ironed Royal Mail uniform
and a digital watch, stands in front of a cooker. He
holds the egg-timer in his left hand and an egg in his
right. There is a saucepan of boiling water on the
hob. PETE'S gaze is fixed on a huge clock, which hangs
on the wall of his small, open-plan flat. Through a
window behind him, we see that it is dark outside.

CLOSE-UP: THE CLOCK - THE SECOND HAND WILL HIT TWELVE
O'CLOCK IN PRECISELY THREE SECONDS. THE TIME WILL THEN
BE TEN MINUTES PAST FIVE.

As the second hand hits twelve, PETE turns over the
egg-timer, and sets it down on the worktop, whilst
simultaneously dropping the egg into the saucepan.

> PETE (V.O.)
> The American politician, Colin
> Powell, once said; 'If you are
> going to achieve excellence in big
> things, you develop the habit in
> little matters.'

PETE checks his watch, and then turns towards a
fridge, which has a large whiteboard attached to the
door. Drawn onto the whiteboard is a chart entitled
'WEEKLY SCHEDULE'. The vertical axis lists the seven
days of the week. The horizontal axis lists one
hundred routine activities, accompanied by the time of
day that each task should be carried out.

PETE unclips a marker pen from the whiteboard, and
puts a tick beside an activity from Wednesday's
column, which reads: '5.10 - BOIL EGG'. We also see
the two entries below this, which read '5.11 - BOIL

KETTLE', and '5.12 - FEED JOSS'.

                    PETE (V.O.)
          My name is Pete Thompson, and I've
          developed the habit.

PETE turns to one of the kitchen cupboards. He opens
the cupboard and removes a mug and a tea bag. He turns
back towards the clock.

CLOSE-UP: THE CLOCK - THERE ARE STILL THIRTY SECONDS
TO GO UNTIL THE TIME HITS 5.11.

PETE drops the tea bag into the mug, and then checks
his watch, before opening another cupboard, from which
he removes a tin of dog food.

Just as PETE produces the tin from the cupboard,
JOSS, a black labrador, enters. She carries a bicycle
helmet in her mouth by its strap. JOSS puts the helmet
onto the seat of a chair, and then sits down on a mat
beside the kitchen table. On her mat, there is an
empty bowl labelled 'DOG'.

Still holding the tin of dog food, PETE ignores JOSS,
and freezes once again, staring at the clock.

CLOSE-UP: THE CLOCK - THE SECOND HAND WILL HIT TWELVE
O'CLOCK IN THREE SECONDS.

PETE moves towards the kettle, and puts his finger on
the switch.

                    PETE (V.O.)
          That's my dog, Joss. She's developed
          the habit too.

As the time hits 5.11 exactly, PETE flips the switch of
the kettle. He opens a kitchen drawer, and removes a
tin opener, which he uses to open the tin of dog food.
He takes an egg-cup out of a cupboard, and puts it

onto a plate. PETE checks his watch, and then removes
a block of butter from the fridge.

He begins to butter three slices of bread. Finding
the butter difficult to spread, he starts to panic
slightly. As he tries to speed up, his eyes flash back
and forth between the hands of the clock and the sand
seeping down through the egg timer. As he checks his
watch again, his action becomes more vigorous - the
knife making holes in the bread. He gives up on the
third slice, and tosses it into the bin.

PETE cuts the other two slices into soldiers before
moving towards JOSS with the tin of dog food, and
picking up her bowl. JOSS stands up, and turns to face
the clock. She begins to wag her tail. PETE stands
beside her, staring at the clock. He holds the tin up
to the bowl, ready to tip out the contents.

CLOSE-UP: THE CLOCK - THE SECOND HAND WILL HIT TWELVE
O'CLOCK IN TWO SECONDS.

As the time hits 5.12, JOSS lets out a single bark,
and PETE tips the dog food into the bowl. JOSS turns
around, ready to eat. PETE checks his watch, and then
puts the food down in front of her.

As JOSS eats her breakfast, PETE turns back to the
fridge and ticks off another two entries on the chart.
We see that the following three entries read: '5.15
- EAT BOILED EGG', '5.19 - DRINK TEA', '5.22 - PUT ON
HELMET'.

CUT TO:

2. EXT. MAIN ROAD, LEEDS - HALF AN HOUR LATER

Daylight is breaking, as PETE, now wearing his helmet,
and with a postbag over one shoulder, cycles along a
busy road towards a set of traffic lights. He sticks
his arm out to indicate left.

                    PETE (V.O.)
          As my good friend, Mr Powell,
          understood, the trick to achieving
          success in life is two-fold.

CLOSE-UP: A ROAD SIGN FOR 'ROYAL MAIL SORTING OFFICE'
POINTS TO THE LEFT.

                    PETE (V.O.)
          First, a man must devise a routine.

Just as PETE reaches the lights, they turn red. He
stops in the centre of the road, with a long queue of
traffic behind him.

He lifts his left wrist to check the time on his
watch.

CLOSE-UP: PETE'S WATCH - THE TIME IS 5.44 AND
50 SECONDS

                    PETE (V.O.)
          Second, he must stick to it.

The traffic lights change to green. PETE doesn't move,
but continues to stare at his watch.

The DRIVERS of the vehicles behind him honk their
horns. Two cars drive around him.

                    PETE (V.O.)
          No matter who stands in his way.

CLOSE-UP: PETE'S WATCH - THE TIME FLICKS TO 5.45 AND
ZERO SECONDS.

PETE drives through the traffic lights, and turns off to
the left.

                                        CUT TO:

3. EXT. SORTING OFFICE - TWO MINUTES LATER

PETE dismounts his bicycle beside a large, grey
building, which has a Royal Mail logo on the side.
Various other POSTAL WORKERS are also arriving; some
in vehicles and others on foot.

As PETE chains his bicycle to a railing, a small white
truck enters the building's grounds. The truck is in
need of a wash, and has various gardening tools in the
back. It has writing stencilled on both sides, which
reads 'MIKE GREEN GARDENING SERVICES'.

As the truck pulls up behind him, PETE looks up and
catches the eye of a woman in the passenger seat,
who is looking, pensively, out of the window. This is
SAMANTHA, 30 and attractive with dark hair tied into a
pony tail. She also wears a Royal Mail uniform.

Noticing PETE, SAMANTHA makes eye contact with him
for a moment. As PETE looks away, she appears a
little guilty. She watches PETE remove his helmet,
while beside her, the driver of the truck talks in
an animated manner. This is MIKE, 35, and rugged in
appearance. He wears a checked shirt over a dirty vest
top and jeans. He appears to be complaining.

CONTINUOUS:

4. INT. MIKE'S TRUCK

                    MIKE
          So, I told him. I'm not doing it for
          any less than three hundred.
                    (beat)
          Are you even listening?

                    SAMANTHA
          What?

MIKE peers out of the windscreen to see what SAMANTHA

is looking at.

MIKE'S POV: PETE is standing beside his bike,
with his helmet tucked under his right arm. He holds
his left arm up in a pronounced position; his elbow
sticking out, as he stares at his watch. He appears
perfectly still, like a robot who has just had his
power source removed.

                    MIKE
          Look at that pillock.
          What's he doing?

SAMANTHA removes her seat belt.

                    SAMANTHA
          Are you still coming with me tonight?

                    MIKE
               (still focused on PETE)
          Huh?

                    SAMANTHA
          To visit Dad.

                    MIKE
          I'll see how it goes.

SAMANTHA gets out of the truck, and closes the door.

                              CUT TO:

5. INT. SORTING OFFICE - LATER THAT MORNING

PETE sorts letters by placing them into various pigeon
holes. He works silently, at a steady pace, pausing
occasionally to check the time on his watch. Around
him, colleagues can be heard laughing and chattering
as they work.

ERIC, 25, with scruffy hair and a creased uniform,

approaches an ancient-looking coffee machine, which
stands against the wall behind PETE.

                    ERIC
          Fancy a beer tonight, Pete?

                    PETE
          (without looking up)
          Sorry. No time.

As ERIC takes his coffee and begins to drink it,
SAMANTHA approaches the machine and presses one of
the buttons.

                    SAMANTHA
          Damn.

                    ERIC
          Problem?

                    SAMANTHA
          I don't think it's working.

                    ERIC
          Allow me.

ERIC sets his cup down, and then gives the machine
a kick. A cardboard cup drops out and starts filling
with coffee.

                    SAMANTHA
          Thanks.

As SAMANTHA picks up the cup, ERIC notices a ring on
her engagement finger.

CLOSE UP: THE RING - IT IS A GOLD BAND WITH THREE RUBY
STONES. IT LOOKS LIKE AN ANTIQUE.

                    ERIC
          Nice rock you've got there.

Hearing this, PETE looks up, and sees the ring on
SAMANTHA's finger.

> SAMANTHA
> Yeah, Mike and I, we ...

ERIC glances in PETE'S direction. Realising that PETE
is watching, SAMANTHA looks embarrassed.

> SAMANTHA (CONT'D)
> Thanks for the coffee.

As PETE checks his watch, SAMANTHA walks off. ERIC
picks up his coffee cup, and returns to his work
station, patting PETE on the shoulder as he passes
him by.

> CUT TO:

6. EXT. RESIDENTIAL AREA - LATER THAT MORNING

PETE cycles past a row of houses. His postbag is full.

CLOSE-UP: A FEW METRES AHEAD, A NAIL STICKS UP IN
THE TARMAC.

As PETE checks his watch, he cycles over the nail,
without noticing. The nail becomes embedded in his
front tyre.

> CUT TO:

7. EXT. PETROL STATION - LATER

PETE is crouched down at the side of the forecourt,
using an air pump to reinflate his bicycle tyre.
Behind him, vehicles are coming and going. PETE checks
his watch.

A MECHANIC, 40, wearing greasy overalls, approaches.
He hands PETE a roll of duct tape.

                         MECHANIC
           If you hang on ten minutes, I'll
           change that for you.

                           PETE
                      (still pumping)
           Thanks, but this will have to do.

The MECHANIC walks away.

                         MECHANIC
           Cheapskate.

As PETE continues pumping, he doesn't notice MIKE'S
truck driving onto the forecourt. The truck stops
beside one of the petrol pumps. MIKE gets out of the
driver's side and starts to refuel.

PETE finishes pumping. He pulls the nail out of
his tyre, and tosses it a few metres away, before
resealing the hole with three pieces of duct tape.
Behind him, we see MIKE heading into the shop to pay
for his fuel.

PETE gets on his bike, and is about to ride off, before
realising that he is still holding the roll of duct
tape. Seeing nowhere to leave it, he looks around for
the MECHANIC, and finally spots him inside the shop.

PETE'S POV: THE MECHANIC STANDS AT THE SERVICE DESK,
BUYING A PACKET OF MINTS.

                                        CUT TO:

8. INT. PETROL STATION SHOP - A FEW SECONDS LATER

PETE enters the shop, intercepting the MECHANIC, who
is about to exit.

                    PETE
            (handing the tape over)
        All done.

                    MECHANIC
        Cheers.

The MECHANIC exits. PETE is about to follow, but then
pauses, as he hears MIKE'S raised voice.

                    MIKE
        Just try it again, will you?

PETE turns to see MIKE standing at the service desk.
The female SALES ASSISTANT, 20, is holding out a Visa
card, waiting for MIKE to take it.

                    SALES ASSISTANT
        I've already tried it twice, sir.
        Perhaps you have another card.

MIKE snatches the card from her hand.

                    MIKE
        I've got some cash in the truck.
        I assume you'll take that.

                    SALES ASSISTANT
        Of course, sir.

As MIKE stomps out of the shop, PETE ducks behind a
shelf, so that MIKE doesn't see him.

                                        CUT TO:

9. EXT. PETROL STATION - CONTINUOUS

PETE exits the shop, keeping his eye on MIKE, who
returns to his truck. MIKE'S colleague, RALPH, 19,
shabbily dressed, with a gormless look about him,
sticks his head out of the passenger door window.

                        RALPH
                Did you get me fags?

As PETE checks his watch and gets onto his bicycle,
MIKE approaches the truck and opens the passenger door.

                        MIKE
                Where's that cash you got yesterday?

PETE starts to ride off. He must pass by the driver's
side of MIKE'S truck to exit.

                        RALPH
                From the old woman's house?

                        MIKE
                Keep your voice down!

Overhearing MIKE'S exclamation, PETE steers his
bicycle back around in a loop, and stops behind a
parked car, out of sight of the two men. He listens
intently, as their conversation continues.

                        RALPH (O.C.)
                  (low)
                Willow Terrace Road, yeah? Fifty
                quid. It's in here.

RALPH opens the glovebox, and passes a bundle of
rolled up bank notes to MIKE.

                        RALPH (CONT'D)
                Did well out of that one.
                  (beat)
                What did Sam think of the ring?

PETE appears concerned, as MIKE counts out some money.

                        MIKE
                Went nuts for it, didn't she?
                Thought it were new.

CLOSE-UP: PETE REACTS.

> RALPH (O.C.)
> Told you she would.

MIKE returns the rest of the money to the glovebox, and closes the passenger door.

> MIKE
> Back in a minute.

As MIKE walks off towards the shop, PETE checks his watch again, and then cycles off.

> CUT TO:

10. INT. SORTING OFFICE - THE NEXT MORNING

PETE sorts letters at the pigeon holes. He looks at his watch, as ERIC appears, riding a child's toy scooter.

> ERIC
> Break time, Pete. You know what
> that means.

CLOSE-UP: PETE'S WATCH - THE TIME IS 8.14 AND 57 SECONDS.

PETE remains frozen for three seconds, as ERIC performs a scooter trick.

CLOSE-UP: PETE'S WATCH - THE TIME FLICKS TO 8.15.

PETE drops the pile of letters in his hand, and walks off.

> ERIC
> (calls after him)
> Come on, man. We've only got
> ten minutes.

                                        CUT TO:

11. INT. SORTING OFFICE - CONTINUOUS

PETE approaches SAMANTHA, who is busy loading her
postbag with mail. A couple of young, female POSTAL
WORKERS reach her before him. They are on their way to
the staff room.

                    POSTAL WORKER 1
          You coming, Sam?

                    SAMANTHA
          Yeah, I just ...
               (noticing PETE)
          Actually, I think I'll stay here. I
          need to reduce my caffeine intake.

                    POSTAL WORKER 2
          She's on a health kick now, ain't
          she? Got to fit into that dress in
          a month.

PETE REACTS - HE IS CLEARLY WORRIED TO LEARN THAT THE
WEDDING IS SO CLOSE.

                    POSTAL WORKER 1
               (clocking PETE)
          We'll see you later, then.

The POSTAL WORKERS walk off towards the staff room,
leaving PETE and SAMANTHA alone.

                    SAMANTHA
          About yesterday. I wanted to tell
          you myself.

ERIC appears, with a cut to his forehead.

                    SAMANTHA (CONT'D)
          Eric? What've you done now?

ERIC holds up the scooter, which is slightly bent.

>ERIC
>D'you know where the first aid kit is?

>SAMANTHA
>Come here. Let me see to you.

SAMANTHA takes the scooter from ERIC, and hands it to
PETE. As she leads ERIC away, PETE checks his watch.

CLOSE-UP: PETE'S WATCH - THE TIME IS 8.16 AND
30 SECONDS.

>SAMANTHA (O.C.) (CONT'D)
>What did I tell you? Eight years
>and under.

>CUT TO:

12. INT. SORTING OFFICE - SEVEN MINUTES LATER

CLOSE-UP: PETE'S WATCH - THE TIME IS 8.23 AND
15 SECONDS.

PETE paces anxiously, as SAMANTHA returns.

>SAMANTHA
>Sorry about that. At least that
>should teach him not to ...

>PETE
>We've only got two minutes, so I'm
>just going to say it.

>SAMANTHA
>Say what?

Behind the Scenes with ... Ashley Pharoah

In 2011, Ashley Pharoah was made an Honorary Fellow of the National Film and Television School in recognition of his outstanding contribution to the British film and television industry. He is the co-creator of the International Emmy Award-winning drama series *Life on Mars*, in addition to its spin-off series, *Ashes to Ashes*. He has also created and written original drama for ITV1, and is the co-founder of Monastic Productions, which was formed in 2006.

The following interview with Ashley was conducted in 2011 by MA Scriptwriting student, Rob Jennings.

We are taught that it is vital to develop your own distinct voice and presentational style. If you read a piece of work that 'stood out from the crowd', would it deter you that the writer had no credits to his/her name?
Depends what the job was. Although you have to remember that I'm not a production company in the classic sense, more a creative rights company. I only really read other writers' work when looking for a series writer. I would expect to see some blindingly original work, but also it would be helpful if there was some sort of track record. Series television is a tough place to work, and not a place to learn on the job. That is what short films are for, and series like *Doctors*. Ironically, it's probably in the film business where a completely new writer *might* be picked up, if they'd written a movie script that people really wanted to make.

What would your advice be to fledglings who are fresh from university, and preparing for a career in scriptwriting?
My advice would be to write. A lot. All the time. Read scripts of films/series that you admire. Try and isolate what makes them good. Watch movies and TV. Consider making short films; so cheap to do these days (lots of festivals etc).

What do you look for in a 'something special' script?
Both a freshness of touch and feel and also an awareness of craft and genre. You just know when you're reading a script by a skilled screenwriter. Each scene is surprising, tantalising. If you want to know what I mean, read Robert Towne's script for

Chinatown. Feel his amazing control, how he plants seeds and questions.

How many times has someone delivered an impromptu pitch to you in the last six months? And, does that approach really work?
Nobody pitches to me, really, as I don't produce other people's work.

If I were to approach you with an offer to work for nothing for six months, would this sway any decision?
To be honest, I think you'd be wasting six months. In that time, you could write a fresh film script. Create a pilot script for a series. Read. Write. It's not like you want to be a script editor or producer. Nobody will make your scripts because you make good tea!
All they are interested in is your talent, so everything you do must ensure that your talent gets honed. Good luck! It's not the easiest time, but the business is always looking for the Next Big Thing. Keep writing. Try and blag an agent. Keep writing!!!

Behind The Scenes with ... Esther Wilson

Esther Wilson has written for television drama series, such as *Accused*, *Moving On*, and *The Street*, for which she was awarded the Best Newcomer prize at the RTS awards in 2009. For her work on the stage play, *Unprotected*, she won an Amnesty International Freedom of Expression Award, and this production was also broadcast as a radio play on BBC Radio 4.

The following extracts are taken from an interview with Esther, which was conducted in 2011 by MA Scriptwriting student, Shannon Tweed.

I didn't get into writing in the conventional way. I never had this burning ambition to write. I'd been an actress in theatre with a physical theatre company (Kaboodle) for a few years. When the company dissolved (Lee Beagley the director went to work in Europe), I took time out to do a degree. As I'd left school at 15 without any qualifications, was married at 19 and had two wonderful children by the time I was 24, I always felt under-confident about my lack of education. So I went to Liverpool John Moores University to embark on a joint honours degree in Theatre Studies and Imaginative Writing. That's where I started writing seriously. Once I'd graduated I taught for a while. I would write from the devising process for students, so in that way I started to learn my craft. I wrote a few plays for a local organisation, working with a director whom I had an artistic affinity with. To this day she is still the best director I work with (she was also in Kaboodle) when we make work together.

In 2002 (I think it was 2002!) I entered a BBC Northern Exposure competition. The BBC was actively trying to encourage ideas from people in the regions. Five writers from five Northern cities. I won one of the bursaries with a short film treatment *The Swimming Man* ... a story about my grandad in Thirties Glasgow. I clearly didn't know what I was doing as it was far too expensive to make but they saw something in my writing and introduced me to Pauline Harris, a BBC radio drama producer based in Manchester. She gave me my first commission. I also got my first theatre commission around the same time with Red Ladder: *Soulskin*, working with Wendy Harris. Again I was fortunate to work with two great directors.

My first R4 play was called *Hiding Leonard Cohen*. It was about a young working class lad who goes to a top university and gets depressed. His depression impacts on the family. It came from a truthful place. I'd had some experience of it myself with my own family, but also I knew from teaching students that it was a huge problem in our society (still is ... I've just written an episode of *Moving On* for TV on the same subject). It won the best radio drama award at the Mental Health in Media awards. That gave me, and the commissioning editors, more confidence in my work.

So even though the short film treatment was massively flawed in terms of it being too expensive to shoot, it was inspired by a true incident. I had an emotional attachment to it so I treated it with great care. It was set in the Depression when people were desperate, but I wanted it to be beautiful so even though it's about a harsh reality its form is poetic, represented in the language. I'm told that's why the panel chose it as one of the winners. They 'saw something'. Equally, even though *Hiding Leonard Cohen* was about depression, I had to avoid it being depressing. Depression is, of its nature, an insular state of being. People who suffer from it can't see beyond what is happening to them ... which isn't very dramatic, and is boring for people around them. That was my task with it. I was lucky that I had a very experienced producer in Pauline.

I have been lucky all my artistic life to be honest. I've had brilliant, generous artists to learn from and to work with. So I capitalised on an opportunity the BBC was offering and I told stories that were dear to my heart. But there is another, more simple element. Relationships. Think about the people you 'click' with in your life ... you do so for a reason. It's the same in every walk of life. There are directors I couldn't work with in a million years because I don't gel with them as people (and vice versa obviously). So you need to actively be going to workshops to meet people. There will be people who you connect with. Remember producers want to make good work too. We may see these institutions and the people who work in them as somehow 'special'. They're not. Really. That's the single most important lesson I've learned working as a writer. Your stories are important. You just need to forge relationships with like-minded people. More importantly, don't be put off if you meet a lot of people who may not like the way you tell your stories. Have confidence and faith in your voice. In terms of opening doors, if you do well, even the people who wouldn't return your calls before will give you the time of day ... that's just life. It's just the way it is. But I only work with people who I think I can make good work with.

There are a lot of radio plays about and a lot of less conventional ones too. *Unprotected* turned into a series of monologues for radio as it was the best way to tell those women's stories in that form. With *Darleen Fyles*, I'd been commissioned to write a Friday night play about a young woman with learning difficulties who was obsessed with the emergency services (again inspired by a true story). Pauline Harris wanted to work with an actress with learning difficulties that she'd seen in a Mind the Gap production. When we met Donna Lavin, I was blown away by her so I wrote with her in mind. We've improvised around themes with her and Edmund Davies, the actor who plays Jamie ... to get that sense of truth. I suppose that can be seen as unconventional but ... I work like that in theatre (mostly) so it always seems to produce richer work, in my opinion. It's a taste thing. A lot of writers hate it ... it works for me. I'm about to start researching a radio play about a group of homeless people ... and we want to use homeless people in the piece so ... who knows how it will turn out? But it's exciting.

The kind of stories R4 is looking for are stories about people who are marginalised and probably wouldn't listen to R4. That's why the BBC actively seek to encourage people with regional voices as they are always getting criticised for being too RP or 'middle class'. But other than that ... good stories transcend man-made systems ... they are about the human condition and they have 'heart' at the centre of them.

Best piece of writing advice I have ever been given came from Jimmy McGovern when I was tearing the walls trying to get a story right. 'If it was easy, every bugger would be doing it.' It's hard. If you care, it's always going to be hard. Don't beat yourself up about it. It's like everything ... you need to keep grafting. I don't always know when I'm getting something right ... but I always know when I'm getting it wrong. If you surprise yourself, or make yourself laugh and cry, then there's a fair chance it'll have that effect on others. Let trusted mates (honest ones) read your stuff. Get them round for a read through then talk about what worked and what didn't work. But always remember that it's coming from you so you can take or leave other people's opinions. I once took out a whole strand on the say so of a great director to do a script-in-hand read through. But afterwards I knew it was wrong. It was dramatically more immediate, but it lacked heart ... so I put the strand back in.

I've been directly inspired by all sorts of people. Rose Gentle and the women from the peace camp who inspired *Ten Tiny Toes*. Donna Lavin who is a remarkable and wise young woman. Tony Benn, John Pilger. Brian Haw, Freda Kahlo, the mothers who are represented in *Unprotected*, Shelly Stoops a woman in Liverpool who fights for victims of sexual violence. Jimmy McGovern who is a generous man with a huge heart and a sense of justice, Paul Abbot, Alan Bleasdale ... I could go on, but I'd bore you. In terms of my 'career' there have been lots of people but Jimmy McGovern gave me an opportunity to write my first telly ... an episode of a *Prime Time*, high profile, Emmy & BAFTA award winning series. But my work hasn't changed since I first started to write. I've learned some important techniques and how to switch between mediums but I still write what I want to write. Apart from one thing I wrote that I wasn't too proud of. I'm not telling you. Some dramatists I adore ... Shakespeare, Beckett, Pinter, Kushner, Jim Allen, Miller, Martin McDonagh, Enda Walsh, Walt Whitman Simon Armitage. God it's a conservative list. I shan't bore you any further.